FIRST BRETHREN CHURCH LI
NAPPANEE, INDIANA

YO-BIS-358

Graduation: A New Start

compiled by
Robert G. Flood

Graduation: A New Start

1981
The Moody Bible Institute
of Chicago

All rights reserved. No part of this book may be reproduced in any form without permission in writing from the publisher except in the case of brief quotations embodied in critical articles or reviews.

The use of selected references from various versions of the Bible in this publication does not necessarily imply public endorsement of the versions in their entirety.

Text by Robert Flood, except where noted otherwise.

Library of Congress Cataloging in Publication Data
Main entry under title:
    Graduation—a new start.
    Bibliography: p.
    1. College students—Religious life. 1. Flood, Robert G.
BV4531.2.G69   248.8'3   80-27606
ISBN 0-8024-3298-0

Printed in the United States of America

Contents

FREEDOMS

THE GOD WHO IS THERE

Resources for the Graduate

Preface

Graduation week. The hassle for the tassel. You've cleaned all the books out of your school locker. You've turned them in, maybe taken some home and put them on the shelf. Enough of the books for a few months.

Now someone hands you another one.

Your church, your parents, a friend. Nice of them, isn't it?

But this one appears a little different from the rest. No long sections of forbidding gray text. Photos pull you inside. You'll even find a few cartoons. Opening "deck" copy tells you at a glance what each chapter is all about. There's variety. It reads more like a magazine.

The copy heads in the direction you're headed—off to the campus in the fall, or out into the job world.

If you are going on to college, your application likely is in, perhaps even accepted. So this book doesn't spin its wheels telling you what kinds of schools you might choose. For most of you it's too late.

We try to give you a peek at campus life before you get there. But without apology this book takes an earnest Christian view about you and your future. All the career literature you've read, the school catalogs you've perused, and the input of your school counselor may have missed the spiritual dimension entirely, unless you have just graduated from a Christian high school.

The chapter on Christian careers, for instance, may open your eyes to a whole new world you didn't realize existed—options that go far beyond only the pastorate and the mission field.

If you are a Christian, you may wonder how your faith will stand up on the university campus. This book gives you a glimpse of the spiritual dynamic and Christian action that can be an exciting part of your college life, if you make the right moves when you get there.

One unique section within these pages looks at America. It gives you just a taste of

this nation's rich Christian heritage—and some historic drama from yesteryear. You will come away with a new sense of your own "roots" in this land of the free.

Let this book's closing section boost your sense that God is always within reach, as guest contributors like Joe Bayly and Bill Bright talk about atheists, star treks, and the Creator. And you'll close with an original song (get out your guitar) about "The Man Who Always Was."

Finally, don't overlook the selected list of resources on those back pages. You may come up with a valuable find.

You might want to keep this book after all.

THE OUTLOOK

The unknown. It scares you. Can you survive the demands of college? Will there be a job for you out there somewhere? And the right fellow, or the right girl?

What does God really want to do with your life? Will the world fall apart around you—before you get even half a chance? What if you fail?

The following pages will not answer all your questions. But they can help you establish a healthy view of yourself and the world around you. Let these insights also help you view the unknown with confidence, even buoyancy.

Take one day at a time and wait for the master plan to unfold, piece by piece. And if you should fail somewhere along the line, all is not lost. Only the God of the universe can know your personal future and the events to come. Relax a bit. He alone is in control. He is Lord of all.

CHAPTER 1

The Look Ahead

Your high school days have ended. Your emotions are mixed. A tinge of nostalgia. Great relief. A little sorrow. Jubilant cheers!

But the end of one era only launches another. What next? How will you view the future ahead of you?

Let's try a multiple choice:

☐A. *Worry yourself sleepless.* Let yourself stew over the fact that you don't know exactly what you're going to do. Fret about whether or not you will cut it in college. Imagine yourself penniless, sleeping somewhere on a park bench.

☐B. *Fantasize.* You are going to take the college campus by storm. Girls, or guys, will fall all over you. Studies will be a breeze. The first job you land will make you rich.

☐C. *Don't think at all.* Forget the future. Bury all problems under the rug. Have fun today and just hope that everything will work out—somehow.

☐D. *None of these extremes.*

If you checked option *D,* you've made the right start.

Some people spend half of their time in life worrying about things that might happen to them but seldom do. Worrying about the unknown drains you of energy, wastes your time. If the unforeseen does come along, you simply try to handle it as best you can and bounce back.

But that doesn't excuse you from using good foresight, common sense, and clear thinking as you consider your options.

Nor can you get away for very long with inaction, and assume everything will have to turn out OK.

When Mount St. Helens, in the state of Washington, started puffing steam and ash early in 1980, an old lodgekeeper who lived on the side of the mountain refused to budge. This man, Harry Truman, defied the odds, even when all signs of a major eruption intensified. He insisted the mountain would not blow.

Then, on a quiet Sunday in May, a mighty explosion suddenly blew off the top of the mountain, leveled hundreds of square miles of forest, destroyed serene Spirit Lake, and buried Harry Truman's lodge under thirty feet of mud.

Some would admire the old man's daring. But because he ignored the realities, and insisted it couldn't happen, it cost him his life.

You cannot live on inaction.

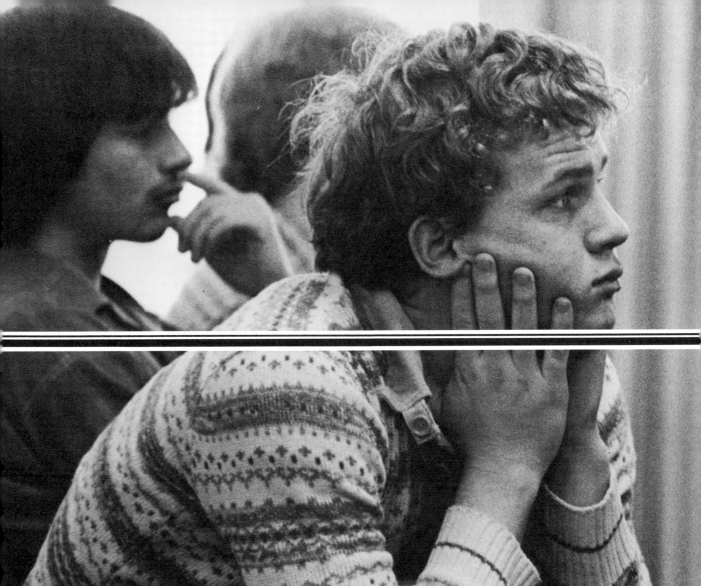

It's time to dispel your fears about the future and step out with confidence into the unknown

Nor on worry and pessimism.

Nor can you live on fantasy—in a dream world that never faces the hard facts and decisions.

But wait a minute. There is a valid place for dreams.

Many never achieve in life all that they might simply because they have never "imagineered" a bit into the future.

They have never entertained any big thoughts, or dreams, or visions—for themselves or for the world around them. They never realize what great things they might accomplish, or what they might become as persons.

The greater danger is that you will set your sights too low, not too high. Or that you will never establish any clear goals at all—that you'll just drift. So go ahead and dream awhile but keep your feet on the ground.

Most who dream about the future will try to shape those dreams into happy ones.

That's natural. But what, really, is "happiness?" A pretty girl, or a handsome guy? A flashy sports car? Athletic honors? Financial success?

John Stuart Mill, an English philosopher, once wrote:

"Those only are happy . . . who have their minds fixed on some object other than their own happiness; on the happiness of others, on the improvement of mankind, even on some art of pursuit, followed not as a means, but as itself an ideal end. Aiming thus at something else, they find happiness by the way."

As you look around you, and think about it, he's right.

But then didn't Jesus remind us of that very truth long before Mill?

"If you cling to your life, you will lose it, but if you give it up for me, you will save it" (Matthew 10:39).

How strange, isn't it, that the One whom we sometimes try to avoid for fear He will spoil our own plans, or stifle our style, is the very One who ever stands by, ready to give us genuine happiness, joy, and an abundant life!

Happy dreams as you ponder your future.

13

by Stanley Mooneyham

What If Your World Falls Apart?

I have met young people immobilized by fear of the future. Nothing seems worth doing, because the world may fall apart in the middle of the doing. Christians are more shaken than they have any right to be. Faith equates with confidence, not with fear. Scripture does not authorize Christians to cringe or cower.

For one thing, there is no stormproof shelter that offers physical security. Where would you take cover to escape apocalypse?

For another, there is the magnificent conclusion of Romans 8. You remember how Paul said it:

"For I am persuaded that neither death, nor life, nor angels, nor principalities, nor powers, nor things present, nor things to come . . . shall be able to separate us from the love of God, which is in Christ Jesus our Lord."

Only recently I rediscovered what I think is one of this passage's most important and neglected phrases:

"Nor things to come."

This means things to come at any time. After death? Sure, but before death, too. Things like an energy shortage. Inflation. International turmoil. Things that happen in Washington, Moscow, Teheran, Afghanistan, wherever. Things that happen on our own street, in our own family, in school or on the job.

Things to come, whatever they may be, hold no paralyzing terror for those whose Lord is Christ Jesus. God's love does not come and go. He will not let anything get in its way.

These four little words, "Nor things to come," restore our perspective, cool our feverish self-centeredness, unclench our fists, straighten our backs, get us going again.

Things present we somehow cope with, however distressing. Nine-tenths of fear hides in the future tense. Fear lives not in the known but in the unknown. Not in what is already here but in what hasn't yet arrived. But note: "Neither . . . things present, nor things to come."

FIRST BRETHREN CHURCH LIBRARY
NAPPANEE, INDIANA

Faith is always for the unexplored place, the experience we have not yet had. Faith is the force that starts our blood circulating, our energies flowing, our thoughts and feet and hands moving. Abraham "went out, not knowing whither he went." What he did know was with whom he went. That was enough.

That doesn't turn a Christian into a Polly-anna; but it should make one an unwavering optimist.

It's *every* Christian's birthright.

Excerpted with permission from *World Vision* magazine, October 1979.

15

CHAPTER

Graduation

Goodbye, little cobweb; goodbye, gym socks; goodbye, little dustballs; goodbye, chewing gum wrappers; goodbye . . .

Football players.

Wake up, Dennis. High school's over.

The Class of '78 left a flagpole. The Class of '79 left a bank of trees. And our class, the respectable Class of 1980, would like to just *leave*.

3 Another Chance

On New Year's Day, 1929, a University of California football player named Roy Riegels made Rose Bowl history. He was playing defense when an opposing Georgia Tech player dropped the ball. Roy grabbed the fumble and took off on a gallop for the end zone. The wrong end zone.

For a moment, all the other players froze. Then, one of Roy's own teammates, Benny Lom, took off in pursuit. After a spectacular fumble return of 65 yards, Lom caught and downed the confused Riegels just before he scored for his opponents.

California took over the ball with their backs to their own goal line. Tech's defense refused to give and California had to punt. But Georgia Tech blocked the kick in the end zone and scored a two-point safety (which was the ultimate margin of victory).

That wrong-way run came shortly before the end of the second quarter. And as the teams left the field at halftime, everyone watching the Rose Bowl that day was wondering the same thing: "What will California coach, Nibbs Price, do with Roy Riegels in the second half?"

The California players silently filed into the dressing room and found places to sit, on benches and on the floor. All of them except Riegels. He wrapped a blanket around his shoulders, sagged to the floor in the corner, put his face in his hands, and cried like a baby.

Football coaches usually have a great deal to say to their teams during halftime. But that day Coach Price was quiet. No doubt he was trying to decide what to do with Riegels. Finally, the timekeeper stuck his head in the dressing room and announced: "Three minutes till playing time."

Coach Price looked at his team, glanced over at Riegels and said simply, "Men, the same team that played the first half will start the second."

The players stood and moved quickly for the door. All but Riegels. He didn't budge. The coach looked back and called to him again: "Riegels." Still he didn't move.

Photo/ Dejected Roy Riegels in 1929 Rose Bowl.

From one of the most famous football games in history: a lesson for those who sometimes fail

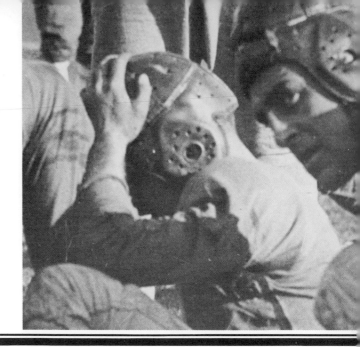

Coach Price walked slowly over to the corner, looked down, and asked softly, "Roy, didn't you hear me? I said, 'The same team that played the first half will start the second.' "

Roy Riegels lifted his head. His eyes were red, his cheeks wet. "Coach," he said, "I can't do it. I've ruined you. I've ruined the University of California. I've ruined myself. I couldn't face that crowd in the stadium to save my life."

Coach Price reached out, put his hand on the player's shoulder, and said to him, "Roy, get up and go on back; the game is only half over."

Roy Riegels went back out on that field. And the Georgia Tech players said afterwards that they'd never seen anyone play as hard as Roy Riegels played that second half.

When I think of this story, I think, "What a coach!"

And then I think about all the big mistakes I've made in life and how God is willing to forgive me and let me try again. I take the ball and run in the wrong direction. I stumble and fall and am so ashamed of myself that I never want to show my face again. But God comes to me and bends over me in the person of his son, Jesus Christ, and he says, "Get up and go on back; the game is only half over."

That is the gospel of the second chance. Of the third chance. Of the hundredth chance.

And when I think of that, I have to say, "What a God!"

© 1978 by Christian Medical Society. Used by permission.

Author Unknown

Lord of All

Christ is the Lord of the smallest atom,
Christ is the Lord of outer space,
Christ is the Lord of the constellations,
Christ is the Lord of every place;
Of the farthest star,
Of the coffee bar,
Of the length of the Berlin Wall,
Of the village green,
Of the Asian scene,
Christ is Lord of all.
Christ is the Lord of the human heartbeat,
Christ is the Lord of every breath,
Christ is the Lord of man's existence,
Christ is the Lord of life and death.
Christ is Lord of our thoughts and feelings,
Christ is Lord of all we plan,
Christ is the Lord of man's decisions,
Christ is the Lord of total man;
In the local street where people meet,
In the church or the nearby hall,
In the factory
In the family
Christ is Lord of all.
Christ is the Lord of our love and courtship,
Christ is the Lord of man and wife,
Christ is the Lord of the things we care for,
Christ is the Lord of all our life.

THE CAMPUS

The university. A big, sprawling complex. Buildings everywhere. Bicycles lined up. Students racing all directions during change of classes, like frantic ants on a busy work project.

Or a quiet campus, almost hidden away in a small town. Maybe almost too small. And it's a long way from home.

Or the community college across town. No big exotic adventure. You've been by it many times. And you'll be living at home, anyway.

But there's so much to do. Two term papers already assigned, and a test in Psychology 102 the second week! You know it's going to get much heavier. Time will run out. What should be your priorities? In studies? Social life? You mean there's really time for the spiritual?

The first week you meet two "out-front" Christians. They're not hiding in the woodwork, that's for sure. Maybe you don't want to, either. That weekend Christian retreat they invited you to sounds like it might be fun.

Decisions.

You wonder: Will you really have the courage in this place to be out in the open about your faith—if someone presses you?

Or even if they don't?

CHAPTER 4

College May Be Possible After All

If you are headed for the college campus this fall, your application likely is in, perhaps even accepted. That means for most of you it is too late to overwhelm you with a lot of data on how to choose a college.

But if you have dismissed the idea of college simply because you think your grades are not good enough, or there is no way you can afford it, you may have thrown in the towel too early.

In her article "Finding Your Way Through the College Maze" (September 1980, *Moody Monthly*), Janet Neidhardt points out some facts that may prompt you to take another last-minute look at your options.

"Some people think you have to be a top student to get into college," she says. "This is not so." At least, not at many schools, both secular and Christian.

In a survey of more than one hundred Christian colleges, for instance, she asked the question, "Do you admit many students with B minus or C plus average in high school?"

Some 66 percent of the Christian liberal arts colleges and 85 percent of the Bible schools responded, "More than a few."

On the whole, Christian colleges, she found, consider the following factors in order of importance for admission: high school grades (and/or rank in class), S.A.T. scores, Christian commitment, recommendation, leadership, interview, and extracurricular activities.

"A student could have only average grades (C plus) *or* low recommendations and/or Christian testimony," she says, "and be accepted at several good Christian colleges."

And in the same article Janet Neidhardt says "More than one hundred accredited Christian liberal arts colleges and another seventy Bible colleges and institutes are educating young people for a multitude of careers."

Although many of those schools may not have the kind of broad curriculum that one would find at a university, the quality of

You may still be able to swing it, even if you don't have top grades or a lot of money lying around

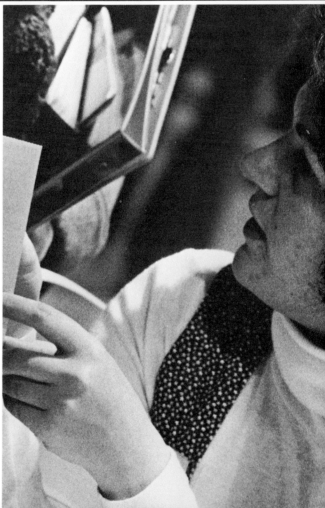

education often is high within those fields in which the schools do specialize.

And you will be getting a thoroughly Christian point of view that secular educators not only omit but often even contradict.

There was a time in the history of our nation when the Christian view prevailed in education. When you read later in this book of how Christians founded the Ivy League (see p. 00), you may realize for the first time that any student in a good Christian college is in the very best tradition of early higher education in America. That education was centered in Jesus Christ, and what could be more important? The Scripture says it powerfully—that in Jesus Christ "are hidden all the treasures of wisdom and knowledge" (see Colossians 2:3).

The "revival" of Christian higher education in America continues to surprise (even alarm) educators who thought they had shoved the idea of God to the sidelines and replaced it with secular humanism. Still, the majority of

college-bound high school graduates will find themselves on secular campuses, and the chapters that immediately follow speak to this challenge. Read on and learn how you can help bring Jesus Christ into that academic scene.

For those who have chosen a Christian school, one word of caution.

Don't assume that the spiritual climate of the school you've selected, however great it may be, will automatically make you—or keep you—a vibrant Christian. The school alone can never substitute for your own personal devotional life or walk with the Lord on a day-to-day basis.

In fact, as you absorb so much spiritual truth, you'll have to look for ways to share it, and use it, and put it to work, so that you don't go "flat" in your spiritual life.

Don't assume either that, because the campus is a "Christian" one, you will find everyone there "fully committed." Some Christian schools, by design, admit a few non-Christian students or "nominal" Christians. You will probably find the highest level of commitment on the campus of a Bible institute. Yet on any Christian campus some students seem to "have it all together," and others may not.

And when it comes to "getting it all together," what about the money problem?

If grades haven't thrown you a major blow or a mental block in your thoughts about a college career, maybe finances have.

But are you sure that money has to shut you out? If you have not explored thoroughly all the financial angles (some of them capsuled at the right), you may be closing the door on yourself prematurely.

Yes, college may be possible for you after all.

by Janet Neidhardt

Meeting the High Cost of College

Many students say, "I can't afford to go to college." With the rocketing costs, most of us probably believe that. However, according to high school guidance counselors and recent newspaper and magazine articles, you can afford college because of the many ways of receiving financial assistance. Briefly, types·of financial aid are:

Scholarships: Usually for students with very good grades (3.5) and low family income, but lately middle income families are qualifying for such scholarships.

Grants: Students without top grades can qualify for grants if in a low or middle income bracket. (Inquire about Middle Income Student Assistance Act (federal money) and Basic Educational Opportunity Grants (BEOG program) at your school financial aid office.

Loans: Guaranteed Student Loan Program provides loan money at 7 percent interest payable after college is completed. The National Direct Student Loan program provides money at 3 percent interest payable after college is complete.

Part-time jobs: Work on and near campus can provide an average of $900 during the school year.

Summer jobs: Can provide $1,000 or more depending on wage scale and skill.

To find out about aid, ask high school counselors for F.A.F. (Financial Aid Forms), a brochure entitled *Meeting College Costs,* and all specific grant and loan information.

Another way to beat the high cost of college is to utilize the local community college and then transfer to the college of your choice. If this is planned carefully, up to sixty credits can be transferred (provided grades are good and courses are correct). . . .

Using this method, a family can save from $6,000 to $8,000 in two years and still have the degree from a well-known college.

CHAPTER 5

Behind the Campus Ivy

If you are a Christian headed for a secular university, what can you expect ahead?

Will your days on campus turn into a dream? Or a nightmare?

Will you find other Christians behind the campus ivy?

Can you still hold to the gospel in the classroom and not commit intellectual suicide?

These are some of the questions that worry you.

Let's be frank. Some church-reared kids fall out of the Lord's ranks soon after they hit the university campus. Embarrassed to identify as a Christian, or bent on pleasure at any cost, they promptly blend into the scenery and conceal themselves better than an army camouflage job.

But some of them were never real Christians in the first place. They only pretended to be.

How you handle it may well depend on whether or not you find your way into one of the evangelical movements on campus and into a good church nearby.

Without either of those, the risk of becoming a "casualty" rises sharply.

What a tragedy that would be when other students are finding their university years a rich Christian experience.

At the University of North Carolina, for example, some six hundred students turn out weekly for meetings sponsored by the Inter-Varsity Christian Fellowship. And more than one hundred small-group Bible studies exist behind the scenes—in dormitories, fraternities, sororities, and other such unlikely places.

Several hundred miles north at Penn State, a network of more than eight hundred students is at work in evangelism on campus through Campus Crusade for Christ action groups.

But many with church backgrounds simply neglect to take any initiative of their own to find a Christian group, especially if it is not highly visible to them. The typical university is a huge, sprawling complex, and amid scores of buildings, posters, and bulletin boards, you may never "accidentally" discover when or where the Christian groups meet.

The first two weeks on campus are crucial. That's why evangelical groups often set up

The first week you hit the university, search out a good Christian movement on campus and join in

near registration lines, along with many other campus organizations looking for "recruits."

And one of their first fall events may be a weekend retreat—an ideal way for you, as a freshman, to meet new friends and set some spiritual directions at the outset of your college experience.

How do the three major "parachurch" movements on US campuses: Inter-Varsity Christian Fellowship, Campus Crusade for Christ, and The Navigators (see capsule profiles on page 00), differ?

Although it is risky to generalize, a few observations might be made.

Inter-Varsity is the oldest of the movements. Perhaps because of its British roots, it tends to be a little more "intellectual" in its emphasis, and its evangelism is usually a bit low-key.

Its structure tends to be indigenous. That is, the work on campus lies in the hands of students, and usually a roving Inter-Varsity staff worker assigned to a rather large circuit of schools drops by from time to time to counsel and encourage.

Therefore, Inter-Varsity's strength on a given campus tends to ebb or flow with the

strength, or weakness, of the campus leadership.

Over the years Inter-Varsity has imparted to student generations a warm gospel outreach, a reverent hymnology, and a remarkable emphasis on world missions.

The latter is dramatized by its gigantic week-long student missionary conference until recently held every three years at the University of Illinois, Urbana. Because more than eighteen thousand registrants from the US and abroad more than filled the university's capacity during Christmas break in 1979, the next Urbana conference has been advanced to December, 1981.

Campus Crusade for Christ is seen by many to be more flamboyant in its style, and perhaps more aggressive in direct evangelism, using as its point of evangelistic focus "The Four Spiritual Laws."

From the outset of its beginning at UCLA in 1951, when it saw much of the UCLA football team converted, Campus Crusade has stressed a strategy of reaching the campus "elite," or leaders, who in turn could influence the masses.

Though at one time criticized by some for its "selective evangelism," Campus Crusade's rapid growth and vast impact in the last thirty years may point up the validity of its chosen strategy. Today Campus Crusade reaches a broad cross-section of students.

Campus Crusade tends to be highly organized and systematic in its effort to evangelize and disciple. On many campuses —Penn State, for example—workers systematically cover the campus by telephone, setting up casual chats and spiritual counsel by appointment.

A third movement, The Navigators, which began as an outreach to the military, has long majored on discipleship—one on one and in small groups. Its profile on campus tends to be lower, but nonetheless solid, with the goal of seeing converts trained to win others and thus multiply themselves. Basic to its discipleship training is an ambitious Scripture memory program.

Although each of these movements maintains its distinctives, over the years they have tended to borrow some of each others' strengths to correct their weaknesses, with beneficial results to all.

Do you have a choice of all three movements?

On a few campuses, especially larger ones, yes, but more frequently you will find only one or two. And at some smaller schools, especially those who rely heavily on the commuter student, you may find none of them.

What can you do now to prepare for life on a university campus?

Talk to other Christians who have blazed the ivy trail ahead of you. What did they find? What lessons did they learn? What do they wish someone had told them as freshmen?

If you plan to attend the same campus as your friend, can that person put you in contact with a Christian professor, a student, a good Christian organization, a Christian family in the community, a good church nearby?

Dig into a Christian book or two this summer that will challenge your intellect and your heart—perhaps in the field of science, marriage, psychology, or any number of other fields. (See Resources on page 00 for some suggestions.)

Maybe you can be one of the fortunate ones to attend a Christian summer camp geared for those who will be entering college in the fall (write to the organizations already described for information).

The university is a place where you'll be grappling with new ideas. Some will conflict with the Christian view; others will not. You'll have to sift and discern.

If you're openly a Christian, someone sooner or later will accuse you of bias.

And they'll be right. You have certain presuppositions, and those underlie your thinking. But the nonbeliever has his presuppositions too, and he is probably just as biased. That is something he either doesn't realize or doesn't admit.

Those who pride themselves most about being open-minded usually never make up their minds about much of anything. It is popular to seek the truth, but you may be ridiculed if you say you have found it.

Yet behind the critic's bold front, he may only be covering his own doubts and insecurities. In his heart he will probably wish he had your courage and conviction.

If your life backs up what you say, your stand for Jesus Christ will earn respect.

Life on a university campus can broaden your interests, extend your vision, increase your confidence. There too you can learn daily how the non-Christian thinks and how to present Jesus Christ in the kind of language he'll understand.

Don't underestimate the influence you can have as a Christian on a university campus. Across America today hundreds of college students—one by one—are finding Jesus Christ because certain dedicated Christians here and there mean business with God.

Even professors can be moved by those who reveal a purpose in life and whose lives are genuine.

On an Oregon campus some years ago, when a political science professor saw the impact Jesus Christ had made on the lives of some of his students, he was forced to re-evaluate his own conception of Christianity.

Through those students and the outstanding Christian leaders whom they invited to speak on campus, the professor, in his own words, "discovered that real Christianity is not a relationship to an organization—the church—but a relationship to Jesus Christ."

"More and more," this man later wrote, "the great gospel message began to make sense."

That man has now been serving in Congress for many years as Senator Mark O. Hatfield.

It was while editor of the campus newspaper at a state university in California that my own life was redirected by the example of earnest Christians.

In fact, the great world missionary movement of the last century was almost entirely initiated by university students intent on taking the gospel to the ends of the earth.

While on the college campus, don't miss out on the Christian action already underway by your generation.

Profiles of Three Campus Movements

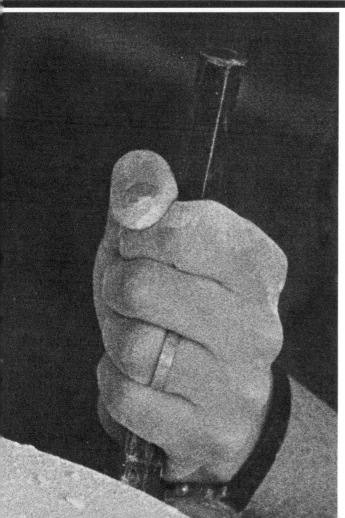

Inter-Varsity Christian Fellowship, USA

History: Has its roots in a student evangelical movement in England in the 1870s, particularly at Oxford and Cambridge universities. It eventually spread to Canada, then into the United States. First local groups formed in Michigan and Washington in 1939.

Campuses: More than 750, including schools of nursing.

Staff: More than 300 full-time. Inter-Varsity majors on indigenous approach, in which students shoulder the main responsibility on campus, with staff members (usually covering many campuses) coming alongside at times to help. Estimated 26,000 students actively involved.

Largest campus groups: East, University of North Carolina; Midwest, University of Minnesota; West, Chico State, California.

National headquarters: 233 Langdon Street, Madison, Wisconsin 53703. Phone: (608) 257-0263.

President: Dr. John Alexander, former professor of geography, University of Wisconsin.

Distinctive ministries: Nurses Christian Fellowship, active in 159 nursing schools. Faculty ministry director: Dr. Charles Hummel. Twentyone-Hundred Productions, traveling evangelistic multimedia show.

Distinctive event: Urbana Missionary Conference (now biannual), University of Illinois, between Christmas and New Year's. The 1979 event drew more than 18,000 registrants.

Special evangelism projects: Fort Lauderdale (Easter). Summer: Aspen, Colorado; Mackinac Island, Michigan; Mexico.

Camps: Catalina Island, California; Bear Trap Ranch, Colorado; Cedar Campus, Michigan.

Magazine: *His*; circulation 25,000.

Publishing house: Inter-Varsity Press.

World outreach: International Fellowship of Evangelical Students (IFES), established in more than 63 countries.

Campus Crusade for Christ

History: The movement began as an inter-denominational student thrust on the campus of UCLA in the fall of 1951 when former Oklahoma businessman Bill Bright and his wife, Vonette, leased a home near the campus and began to tell the students about Jesus Christ.

Campuses: More than 200 (with full-time staff). Student associates on many more campuses.

Staff: Some 1200 in the US.

Largest campus groups: East, Penn State; South, University of Alabama; Midwest, University of Indiana; West, Oregon State.

National headquarters: Arrowhead Springs, San Bernardino, California 92403. Phone: (714) 885-7531.

President: Bill Bright.

Distinctive ministries: Military, high schools, athletes, college faculty, and others.

Distinctive event: Annual one-month Institute of Biblical Studies at Colorado State University, Ft. Collins. Regional "Christmas Conferences" in major American cities.

Special evangelism projects: Numerous beach and resort areas in summer, inner city (Chicago; Washington, D.C.), international students.

Camps: Arrowhead Springs; year-round headquarters complex with excellent facilities. Hosts staff training, family conferences, evangelism seminars, and many other events.

Magazine: *Worldwide Challenge;* circulation 100,000. Also *Athletes In Action,* published quarterly.

Publishing house: Here's Life Publishers.

World outreach: Missionaries in more than 114 countries. Campus Crusade's total worldwide staff, including associate members, numbers nearly 12,000.

The Navigators

History: Founded in 1943 by Dawson Trotman.

Campuses: 140 in the United States. Active in 34 countries.

Staff: 234 full-time. Overseas staff: 1,696.

National headquarters: 3820 N. Thirtieth Street, Colorado Springs, Colorado 80901. Phone: (303) 598-1212.

President: Lorne Sanney; US director, Jack Mayhall.

Magazine: *NavLog;* circulation 60,000.

Publishing house: NavPress.

Photo right/ Headquarters of The Navigators, near Colorado Springs

CHAPTER 6

by George S. Rust

A Search at Harvard

From the moment I drove into Harvard Square in the family station wagon, I could not help but be impressed. I had finally arrived at Harvard University! I was unsure of what my career would ultimately be, but I saw success available in nearly any direction I might choose.

But my initial excitement about being at Harvard began to wear off as I was plunged into the reality of term papers, tests, and grades. Soon the doubts in my mind about what I would be doing with the rest of my life began to grow into a vague lack of purpose.

I suppose that was when my search began. There had to be something more to life than just books or the pursuit of fun. I did not question the prevailing campus philosophies. "They're all just different paths to God."

It was pleasing intellectually to look at life that way. No one was wrong, and everyone was becoming more enlightened every year. Maybe it was enough just to search and not worry about finding any ultimate answers.

Then, it did make a difference. I was home for Christmas when the telephone rang and I got the news.

My roommate had hanged himself in the stairwell of our dormitory.

My mother cried when I told her, and I was embarrassed. I knew I was the one who should be crying, but I was just too dumbfounded.

I did not have any answers. Friends kept asking the question, "Why?" and I kept making up answers. Deep inside, the real question was nagging at me. What was there about my life that made it meaningful?

Was there any ultimate purpose in life? I had to sort it all out. I walked a lot that semester after Christmas—alone and at night. Out of desperation I prayed a simple prayer. "God, show me how to find you." It was a prayer I would repeat many times in the months ahead.

That summer I decided impulsively to transfer from Harvard to the University of Miami.

After a month at the University of Miami I was convinced that I had made the worst decision of my life. I hit rock bottom on a warm night in September. I stood on a waterfront dock, smoking cigarette after

cigarette, staring into the shimmering, moonlit water. Behind me a boisterous party mocked me. I was ready to give up on God and admit that there were no ultimate answers. That was the turning point.

A few days later I moved into a new dormitory and ran into an old high school friend. Andy and I talked about old times, and finally the conversation got around to Jesus Christ. Andy could not keep from bubbling over about how Jesus Christ had changed his life. I was uncomfortable with all this, but I had to admire his courage in risking our friendship to convey the faith that was such a part of him.

I also realized that my biology lab partner was a believer in Christ. Cindy had fewer opportunities to speak to me about Jesus, but she never missed a chance. I could not help but wonder at the "coincidences" that were bringing me into contact with this simple faith in Jesus.

In the next few weeks I began to see that they were not talking about religion; they were talking about God. Here was what I had been looking for! These people were living in vital contact with God! It all seemed so

simple, and even the simplicity of it seemed to fit.

One weekend Andy invited me to a Christian retreat. The Friday evening session showed me how little I knew about the gospel. This group of believers was certainly not fabricating their own private philosophy. They took their gospel straight—no additions, no deletions. In all my experience I had never been told how to find this personal relationship with God that was the essence of the gospel. It was news to me, and it was good news!

There were still some questions in the back of my mind, but I was beginning to understand that I must experience God for myself. That night, alone in my room, I dropped to my knees and prayed. "God, I'll never find all the answers. If this is the way to find you, then show me."

The next day we were given time to think and pray, so I began thumbing through a Bible. I was just flipping the pages, when suddenly they stopped turning, and a verse nearly leaped off the page at me. "I am the way, and the truth, and the life."

39

It was the record of Jesus' words, but I knew it was also God speaking to my heart. I flipped some more pages, and another verse jumped out at me. "See to it, then, that no one makes a captive of you with the worthless deceit of human wisdom . . . for the full content of divine nature lives in Christ." God himself was reaching down and saying, "This is the way, George. Don't be afraid."

I closed my Bible and shut my eyes. "Lord, I know I need you. I know I've sinned against you. Come into my life." In the next few hours I began to realize that something really was different. Bright rays of hope came streaming into my life.

I started to read the Bible and discovered all kinds of things about Jesus and being a Christian. I found answers to some of the questions I had carried with me in my steps of faith toward God. As I prayed I began to get a glimmer of the living God as he really is, and not as I had imagined him to be.

I began to find purpose in my college studies as well. Earlier I had decided to become a physician, but there was no driving force behind my plans. As a believer in Christ, I was able to pray for God's guidance and direction, and he has been faithful in answering my prayer. I soon felt the full power of the mighty God behind me in my pursuit of a medical career.

I still had not become a part of any local church. After all, I reasoned, I had found Christ outside the church, so I saw no real need for it. But my spiritual life reached a plateau, and I knew that something was missing. The next year I began attending a church that seemed to be everything a church should be. Praise God! Since then the church has been an essential part of my growth as a disciple. Here I have been exposed to the entire spectrum of Christian personalities, young and old. The teaching has been accurate and pointed. The spirit has been one of pure love.

As I get to know God better, I am finding a clearer perspective on the events of my life. All the "coincidences" that led to my conversion show the mark of God's hand. He has taken my mistakes and put them together to give my life the deepest possible purpose. The Lord has established my plans in wonderful ways. It amazes me just how much he loves me. He wants the very best for me!

From *Decision* © 1977 by The Billy Graham Evangelistic Association. Reprinted by permission.

CHAPTER 7

Their Right (and Yours) to Persuade

Scene: The University of Nebraska (or almost any other major campus within recent years). Suddenly one day students begin wearing colorful buttons that announce "Josh is Coming." Posters around the campus back up the same promise.

But who is Josh?

Josh McDowell, of course—the roving campus lecturer who in little more than a decade has talked to more than five million college students about the gospel of Jesus Christ.

Josh, the author of such best-sellers as *Evidence That Demands a Verdict* and its sequel, *More Evidence That Demands a Verdict,* used to ridicule the Bible until a Christian professor at a Michigan college challenged McDowell to examine the evidence with both an open mind and an open heart.

When McDowell arrives on campus, crowds sometimes totaling up to ten thousand turn out over a three-day period to hear his lectures on the resurrection of Jesus Christ, biblical prophecy, and "maximum sex."

Before he leaves, some one thousand students or more may turn in comment cards indicating they have either received Christ or are interested in hearing more.

For Christians on campus, McDowell's lectures become wedges that help open up conversation about spiritual matters on the campus at large, bringing it all out into the open.

McDowell skillfully defuses many of the old-hat arguments about 'religion' and the Bible that many nonbelievers parrot without really examining the facts.

As one who has perhaps just graduated from high school, you may not have seen anyone hit students with the gospel so openly and head on. For unless you have enjoyed the privilege of a Christian high school, it was probably taboo to allow such direct evangelism onto your campus.

Resistance happens at the university level, too. McDowell has been shut out of some schools, as in 1980 at the University of Missouri.

But in higher education the climate is more open. Also, there are some important issues at stake that you should know about.

If universities are the bastions of "academic freedom" that they say they are, then you, as

Agnostics, critics, Christians, fence-riders all turn out when these folk come to the campus

a Christian, have "the right to persuade."

Let's take a case in point.

At Northwestern University a few years ago, during Campus Crusade's nationwide evangelistic "I Found It" campaign, there were critics, including some campus clergy, who strongly objected.

In a letter to the *Daily Northwestern* campus newspaper, they cited an eleven-year-old regulation drawn up by a defunct campus Board of Religion, which declared "proselytizing" on campus illegal. They wanted the administration to put a stop to the campaign at Northwestern.

University President Robert H. Strotz responded, saying the Board of Religion's guidelines were never official university policy and that religious groups were free to "proselytize" at the school.

Then he delivered the clincher.

"What kind of university would this be," he asked, "if we were to say that one person cannot persuade another to a point of view?" (Ann Rodgers, " 'Holy War' over at Northwestern University," *Inter-Varsity Branch,* 1 April 1977.)

Ironically, the rowdy and radically-oriented "free speech" movement of the sixties may

have helped pave the way for evangelical Christians.

If a university can open its premises to the vocal proponents of drugs, free sex, and anarchy, it can hardly put the lid on Christians who are convinced they have a better answer.

It was exactly that kind of confrontation, in fact, that launched the ministry of Josh McDowell.

Caught one day in the crossfire of a demonstration of radicals on the University of Texas campus, McDowell succeeded in securing the microphone and diverting the crowd's attention to the issue of Jesus Christ.

When to his surprise the crowd listened in earnest, McDowell knew the time had come for Christians to start speaking up.

John Alexander, president of Inter-Varsity Christian Fellowship, USA, and a one-time professor of geography at the University of Wisconsin, underscores this right. In an interview on "The Christian's Right to Persuade" (*Inter-Varsity Branch*, 1 April 1977), he says:

"Students and faculty must be free to exchange any ideas they choose both publicly and privately. The moment any authority —on the campus or outside of it—says you may use college facilities to talk about "X," but your speakers cannot talk about "Y"—at that moment intellectual freedom begins to crumble.

"If students are fenced off from intellectual freedom regarding religious ideas," he says, "it may not be long until the strong arm of thought control fences them off from intellectual freedom in other ideas as well."

But does that mean the freedom to disrupt?

No. Alexander calls for responsible freedom and condemns the abuse of such freedoms espoused by belligerent agitators who destroy university property and violate the intellectual freedoms of other people.

"Freedom without control," he says, "is anarchy."

When university administrations fully understand this, strong Christian groups can exist and operate with freedom.

Let's look at another interesting example.

For several decades evolutionary thinking has dominated the university scene, unchallenged except for a few voices here and there.

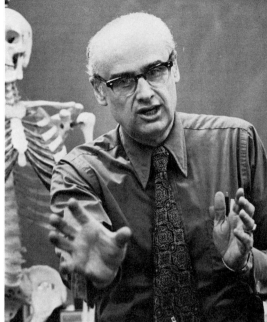

It is no longer so.

Across the country a new breed of scientist has emerged who is fearlessly taking on evolution-oriented scientists in public debate. And in many cases he is pinning his opponent to the mat.

One such figure is Dr. Duane Gish, affiliated with the Institute for Creation Research in San Diego. Crowds sometimes in the thousands jam university auditoriums for those debates.

How do men like Dr. Gish tackle such assignments?

Not with a Bible waving in the air.

Although these men do believe the Bible, they try to meet the issues with scientific evidence alone.

For example, they might demonstrate that the fossil evidence does not substantiate evolution, but in actuality contradicts it.

Or, they may argue the case from the second law of thermodynamics and produce heavy evidence that the universe and all the forms of life it contains demonstrate not upward evolutionary progress, but a constant process of deterioration and decay.

Or, they may cite the laws of probability against the evolutionary thesis.

These debates often expose glaring flaws in evolutionary theory and help to convince some, at least, that scientific evidence argues more strongly for creationism than for evolution.

One of the men in the forefront of the creationist movement has been Dr. John N. Moore, professor of natural science at Michigan State University. Though once an evolutionist himself, he eventually realized that the professors under whom he had sat took one-sided views and shielded him from all the facts.

"Reputable scientists in each decade since Darwin's book was published have been critical of evolution," says Moore. "Why didn't my teachers inform me of that when I was an undergraduate?" (John N. Moore, "Another Choice," Decision, January 1975, p. 3.)

Although the evolutionist may still try to dismiss the creationist view as "religion" and not science, the public is beginning to realize that the evolutionist has created his own 'religion' of sorts, complete with its built-in philosophy of humanism. Simply stated, the creationist puts God at the center; the evolutionist puts man and reason on center stage.

45   Photo right/ Professor John N. Moore, University of Michigan

But the point is that such debates have opened not only a new entree for the gospel but also a fresh breath of academic freedom.

For schools to teach only one "model" of origins—that is, the evolutionary one—is neither good science nor good academics. Why should not every student hear the evidence for both sides, in the open marketplace, and then decide for himself on the basis of the evidence?

Are the creationists making headway?

Yes, says a front-page article in the *Wall Street Journal* (15 June 1979). In this report Dr. Robert Sloan, an evolutionary paleontologist at the University of Minnesota, admitted, "The creationists tend to win" the debates. "Many evolutionists," he said, "concede that the creationists are making progress."

Simply because the creationist may be the best debater?

No, says creationist Dr. Richard Bliss. "We win because the scientific data for the creation model are far better than the evolution model. They regress toward the religious; we stick to the science."

Take courage in one more evangelical thrust on today's university campus. This one is a Dallas-based outreach called Probe.

It is one of the newest efforts to harmonize historic Christian truths with the university's academic disciplines.

At the invitation of Christian groups on campus, it sends out a team of men and women, most of them with advanced degrees, to conduct a week-long Christian Update Forum.

The typical "package" might include twenty-five classroom talks a day, a three-day lecture series for the campus at large, and smaller meetings in dorms, clubs, fraternities, and sororities.

University instructors can choose in advance from a list of about fifty lectures. Topics range from current social issues (energy crisis, ecology, abortion, the occult) and the influence of Christianity on society, to psychology and the nature of man, the physical sciences (evolution vs. creation, the origin of the universe), and the need for moral values in education.

The choice also includes the historicity of biblical documents, an explanation of the Christian world view, and the Christian concept of the free enterprise system.

"One of the most popular talks," says Probe spokesman Bill Rodenberg, "is a discussion on business ethics."

Since the program's inception in 1973, thousands of students have listened to Probe speakers.

How do students react?

With few exceptions, quite favorably.

On the subject of the resurrection and the authority of the New Testament, many students react in surprise at the amount of evidence for the validity of the Scriptures.

"I am not clear in my mind . . . exactly what my religious belief is," one student responded. "However, I am definitely headed to the library today to find out exactly who this man of Nazareth really is.

"So many people have told me what *they* think—I want to establish what *I* think."

Those are just a few of the Christian persuaders active on today's campus—those who, like the apostle Paul, attempt to "persuade men."

If you are a Christian headed for the university, you may have the opportunity to hear these new Christian voices, or even to help invite them onto your campus.

But the most important persuaders of all will be the many "ordinary" Christians on campus, perhaps like you, who will touch the lives of others around you day by day.

JOBS AND CAREERS

You're out of high school now, and this job business is getting serious. Sure, you've mowed lawns and delivered pizzas. But neither of those are exactly ideal lifelong occupations.

The idea of settling into a career scares you. You're not really sure just what you want to do. What if you make the wrong choice, the wrong move? Will you be stuck there forever, always wishing you had trained to be a diplomat to Europe instead of a computer technician?

And the job market seems so tight. Will there be anything left by the time you get out of college? Or will you have to settle for the dregs?

You can dismiss such somber thoughts. New job fields emerge, or expand, every year. And your options down the road will be broader than you think, even if you restlessly change majors. You have lots of latitude, probably even some attractive options that would seem now only remotely related to your major.

Also, God may spring a surprise or two on you along the way, if you'll let Him.

You, a pastor? Not necessarily. A missionary? Maybe. But there's a whole new Christian job market today, too. So read on.

by Matt Huff

CHAPTER 8

Finding the Job in Your Future

When we were young, many people asked what we wanted to be when we grew up. Many boys mentioned "fireman" or "policeman." If you were like me, you wanted to be a house painter or a garbage man! But whatever your childhood dreams, the question of "what do I do when I grow up" needs an answer when school days are over.

If you've been reading the news headlines, you may be wondering if you'll be able to find work at all, let alone work that you like. But statistics can't chart your job life. It's important to know what God wants you to do, and it's important to know what the options are.

How can you know what jobs will be available when you graduate? The "Help Wanted" section of your newspaper will give some clues. There you'll see three basic categories of jobs: college degree, experience only, and "special training."

Going to college with a career plan in mind is helpful. On the other hand, many students discover a new interest in college that leads to a career. Either way, college is

not a bad thing to have; many jobs require a degree before even granting interviews.

Jobs open to college degreed people cover a wide range. Higher education pays off in more ways than wage rates.

"How do I get a job requiring experience when I don't have any?" you may ask. The answer: Look for low-rung jobs that will give you experience. Sales jobs are a good place to start. You'll learn about what you sell, sales techniques, and human nature.

You may be able to find work as a clerk in a store that corresponds with your interests. If you love sports, your enthusiasm as a clerk in a sporting goods store could lead to a better job with more responsibility and a higher salary. If you like to work outdoors, your hard work as a ditch digger for a landscape contractor could lead to a position as a crew chief or as manager of your own landscape company.

Those with more experience fill so many part-time jobs and overtime shifts that desirable jobs are scarce, and you will have to contribute something special to warrant acceptance and advancement. The employer's

Even in a tight job market you can uncover some good options—if you make the right moves

goal is to generate profit, and if you can help him do that, you will be a valued employee.

You don't have to be an employee if you can do something new better than others. Two high schoolers became florists with a quarter-acre plot lent to them. Some college students started their own house painting businesses or catering services to help pay expenses. You have heard about the free enterprise system, but may not realize that you are free to try being as enterprising as anyone else.

As you look through the want ads, you'll see that different jobs require different amounts of training and skills. The same is true for jobs with Christian organizations. If God is leading you to consider a career with one of these, check out what they need and what kind of education or training you'll need.

Unusual occupations are open to young people with special interests. One young person, interested in music, repairs pipe organs. Another who hopes to become an airplane mechanic got his first job at an airplane wrecking company through his high school's work-study program.

If your high school has a job placement service, counselors may help you find your first job. Many employers register with their local high school. School job programs usually include strategies for job-hunting and tips on interviewing that could increase your chances of finding work throughout your life.

If your high school has no such program, your community or junior college may. Cooperative programs between employers and schools are beginning all over North America as employers discover the advantages of testing students before hiring them permanently, and as students find they can try some field before pursuing it further.

If no one near you has a work-study program, some employers will still be looking for capable employees your age; it will just take more persistence to locate them.

Don't be discouraged at turndowns; the job market eventually recognizes a bargain job-seeker.

Reprinted by permission of *Venture* magazine, © 1977 by Christian Service Brigade, Wheaton, Illinois.

CHAPTER

9

Myths That Smother Careers

The Bible makes it clear that we should be good stewards. A more contemporary word is "manager." We manage something (namely, ourselves) which belongs to another (our creator, God). And in managing work, which encompasses the bulk of our waking hours, too many people make choices for careers that are based on false expectations.

Myth #1: I should know exactly what I want to do with my life.

It's natural to assume you should know your career plans. Adults have been asking since your childhood, "What do you want to be when you grow up?" Later they ask, "What are you studying to be?" Generations of adults have confused careers with identity, as if "what you do" is the same as "who you are." At social gatherings, they ask each other, "Who are you?" and what is the answer? A career. "I am a lawyer . . . teacher . . . carpenter. . . ." For many, their identity is their work. Teachers and guidance counselors reinforce the notion: "You must choose now what you will do for the rest of your life."

In reality, you don't have the life experience to make long-range decisions at an early age. Unless, of course, you have some very unusual experiences or potent interests. But few do.

There are more than 21,000 different kinds of occupations. Massive numbers which will someday be available to you have not even been created yet. If you do know what you want to do, great! But if you don't, don't feel guilty or left out.

Your best bet, unless you know exactly what you want, is to prepare yourself for breadth rather than depth. Sample many kinds of courses and experiences rather than focusing on a narrow few. Prepare for adaptability and flexibility.

Myth #2: I should choose what my parents (or friends or counselor or pastor) tell me to do.

There is absolutely nothing wrong with asking for advice. But we must make our own decisions and be responsible for them. To have someone else "hand it to us" makes them accountable for our choices. And if the

Don't be misled by these wrong ideas about the choice of a vocation

choice turns sour, we may blame them, tending to sour relationships.

Parents want the best for their children, yet they are not unbiased, objective parties and may, without even knowing it, be more concerned with what they want for you than for what you want for yourself.

If you follow their wishes, it may make them happy but you may become miserable —which would then make them unhappy and perhaps even guilt-ridden. If you follow what *you* know is best for yourself, it may temporarily disappoint them but they can say, "At least our son/daughter is happy and that's what counts." Make your own decision, since you are the one who must live with the consequences.

Myth #3: I'll run into something. Why worry?

There is a big difference between worrying and planning. Failing to plan is planning to fail.

Actively and purposefully seek out information and options. Interview people about their work. Read and research career information. Don't be limited by ignorance—you can't choose something if you don't know it exists! Learn how to make intelligent decisions. And begin, of course, by personally assessing your needs, values, interests, and talents.

By planning, you may never reach your ideal. But, by happenstance, your chances of reaching that ideal—where "who you are" fits "what you do"—are almost zero.

Myth #4: A test can tell me what I should do.

All a test can do is give you some information about yourself, your aptitudes, personality, and interests. That can be valuable information if you use it properly.

Incidentally, tests are not always properly interpreted. If you do not have a grasp on your self-concept and don't know, by experience, what you enjoy and what you are good at, then a test may give you a starting place for your self-understanding. But no test can unerringly designate your life's work.

Myth #5: I will only make it by getting top grades.

There is very little relationship between grades and success in the workplace, with a few exceptions. Poor grades, to be sure, won't help. But there is something which, to employers, is even more important than grades: experience!

The best career preparation is to participate in jobs, volunteer activities, extra-curricular activities, community service, and Christian work. It doesn't have to be paid experience to be valuable. But it should give you opportunities to take on responsibility, to develop good working habits and attitudes, to gain leadership skills, and to understand how organizations work. Studies show that experiences don't hurt grades; they improve them. Grades can be important, but not at the expense of a variety of experiences. Go for both.

Myth #6: I should choose a career with the best job outlook.

Right now the hottest thing on the job market is petroleum engineers. But what will they do in 20 years when the oil runs out?

The job market changes too quickly to plan ahead for decades. The careers in demand today can be tomorrow's surplus.

The key to career planning is to have a clear second choice and a third choice and a back-up plan if those don't work out. Don't avoid your favorite choice just because of the job market, but don't be blind to the fact that you need to have alternatives at hand.

Myth #7: I need more information about what's "out there."

Only a half-myth. You do need to base your decision-making on information. But more important is knowing yourself. For if what you do is in harmony with who you are, fulfillment is most likely. So instead of starting with what's "out there," begin with what's "in you."

That means coming to grips with "who you are": your vocational interests, your abilities, your psychological needs, your likes and dislikes. It means focusing on what you have done and enjoyed, and how that relates to what you may someday do.

Too many people begin their career planning by asking, "Where do I fit?" Like a peg in a hole. Doesn't it make more sense—even though it is harder work—to discover "what fits me"?

Myth #8: I need to get some skills to be employable.

For some crazy reason, people think of mechanical or technical abilities when they hear the word "skills." Usually they think of skills in terms of working with things. But there are also important skills for working with people and with data.

Ask an executive which skills are the highest level skills in the world of work and he will probably say:

effective communication skills, with both speaking and writing;

interpersonal and human relations skills, getting along with people;

learning how to learn, for there will always be new content to be quickly grasped and digested;

analytical thinking skills, knowing how to turn problems into creative challenges.

Now if you are intending to become a refrigeration mechanic, these skills are not as important as the specific body of information about refrigeration, everything from coils to condensers. But if you anticipate taking your place among the highest level of professions and careers in America, those above-mentioned skills are by far most useful. Often they are obtained en route to a liberal arts education, but never do they come just from taking classes.

Of course, there is no single profession to which they belong. In fact, people with these highest levels of skills could use them in any one of hundreds of possible career opportunities. Hence, they are known as "transferable skills"—they can transfer from one kind of job to another. The content of different careers is easily picked up on the job, but the transferable skills make the difference.

People with specific technical skills do have an easier time getting their first job at the

entry level. But someone with those transferable skills who has a difficult time identifying which career he would like to try will surpass the technician before long in terms of salary, levels of responsibility, and prestige.

Myth #9: I'll probably get stuck in one career.

Nothing could be further from the truth. Not only will you likely change jobs a dozen or so times in your life, but you will probably make 180-degree switches and change careers three or four times in your life. So how can you prepare for multiple careers? By becoming as adaptable and flexible as possible, by learning how to make long-range assumptions about the future, and by enhancing your transferable skills. It is liberating to think that you will not get stuck in one career!

In terms of college, seek education that prepares you for life rather than for one single career, at least at the undergraduate level.

Myth #10: I must become a minister or missionary to serve God full-time.

Serving God is what you do with your life, not just your job. Of course, some choose church occupations. But that is not necessarily the same as ministry—which is an attitude, not a job. It involves those who are ordained and those who are not. It includes those with extensive professional training and those without.

Reprinted by permission from *Group* magazine. Copyright © 1979, Thom Schultz Publications, Inc., Loveland, Colorado.

CHAPTER 10

Today's Amazing New World of Christian Work

In the spring of each year big corporations send recruiters to college campuses and training schools to dangle employment plums before graduating seniors.

Would it surprise you to learn that recruiters from Christian schools and organizations are beginning to do the same?

Take your pick: accounting, bookkeeping, administration, personnel, data processing, purchasing, advertising, public relations, secretarial/office—these are only a few of the opportunities to exercise business skills in the service of Christ.

If God calls you to one of these occupations, you may have the same satisfaction and be in "full-time Christian work" as much as a minister or a missionary.

And wouldn't you rather see your energy expended in advancing the cause of Christ more than some company?

Since the same type work is being performed as in secular office positions, the requirements for corresponding jobs in Christian organizations are similar. Let's look at some examples:

BUSINESS

Data Processors

Today is the age of the computer. And just as secular enterprises have found the computer an indispensable tool in their day-to-day operations, so too have Christian organizations for record keeping, control of inventory, issuing of checks, etc.

The computer revolution has created an acute shortage of engineers, programmers, operators, maintenance technicians and systems analysts. All jobs in computer science require special training. Computer science courses varying in levels of complexity are offered by colleges, technical institutes, business academies, and high school. . . .

Accountants

Accountants who compile and analyze business records and prepare financial reports such as profit and loss statements, balance sheets, cost studies and tax reports can receive training in universities, four-year colleges, junior colleges, accounting and private

Wanted: Secretaries, teachers, data processors, accountants, broadcasters, journalists, and others

by Lowell Saunders

business schools and correspondence schools.

A bachelor's degree with a major in accounting, however, is preferred. . . .

Bookkeepers

Every business firm, Christian or secular, must have systematic and up-to-date records for its financial affairs. Keeping those important records is the job of bookkeeping workers who record daily business transaction.

You'll need to be a high school graduate with courses in business arithmetic and bookkeeping to qualify for one of these positions. It would be better if you completed training in post-high school business education or junior college. If you have above-average aptitude for working with numbers and the ability to concentrate on details, this may be where you will best fit in.

Administrators

Do you think you have a gift for administration? It's possible to work your way up through the ranks to such a position although it would be better to get a college degree in the field. In either case you'll have to be able to weigh various factors intelligently and make good decisions.

Your responsibility as a manager depends on your level of management and type of employer. You may be in a policy making position or you may direct or plan the work of others on a lower level. An increasing number of large churches are employing business managers or administrators to handle their affairs.

Secretaries

It's been said that while administrators make a business succeed, secretaries make administrators succeed. The apostle Paul needed a secretary to take down the letters he dictated, and contemporary church leaders need help, too. Could this be your place of service? . . .

61

Personnel Directors

Every Christian organization faces the problems of attracting and keeping the best employees available and matching them to jobs that they can do efficiently. This is the responsibility of the personnel office. The people in personnel develop recruiting and hiring procedures, interview job applicants and recommend people they feel are best qualified for job openings. And they deal with employee management relations, employee training, and administer employee benefit plans.

Many Christian concerns fill their personnel positions by transferring people who already have firsthand knowledge of the business organization. But you will be better fitted for such a responsibility if you study personnel administration in college, or have a general business administration background.

Promotion

Ever wonder who writes those ads for Christian schools, religious books and publishing houses? Those who have had training in the art of advertising, employed either at the organization itself or with an advertising firm. Among the specialized occupations in this field are advertising managers, account executives, advertising copywriters, production managers, research directors, and artists and layout men. . . .

Your spark of creativity may well have to be developed into a roaring flame for you to succeed in this competitive field. While it's not essential for you to have a college degree, you should have some training in advertising, marketing, journalism or business administration.

COMMUNICATIONS

Print Media

From a human standpoint the invention of printing made the Protestant Reformation possible. The publication of the Bible and the writings of Luther and the other reformers blazed across Europe, ending a millennium of ecclesiastical darkness. "Printing is the last and also the greatest gift of God," said Luther. "By it He wanted to have the cause

of the true religion become known and spread in all languages at the end of the world in all the countries of the earth."

But Luther spoke too soon. In this century the addition of the electronic media—films, broadcasting and television—has given the church the potential of reaching the entire world with the gospel of Christ in a moment of time. Is there a more strategic place for you to invest your life than in some responsibility of the mass media?

In the field of print—books, magazines and newspapers—Christian men and women are urgently needed in writing and production of literature, in editorial responsibility, in marketing, in manning Christian bookstores, in working with graphics, and in overseeing correspondence course work. . . . You can discover your potential in this area and begin your training outside of the college arena by working on a small magazine or newspaper.

Broadcasting

In the electronic media, the several hundred Christian radio and television stations in this country and the scores of overseas missionary stations require thousands of talented people in serving as announcers, producers, writers, newsmen, program personnel, supervisors, musicians, actors, film editors and librarians.

On the technical side of things, broadcast technicians set up, operate and maintain the electronic equipment needed to record and/or transmit radio and television programs. They work with microphones, consoles, sound recorders, lighting equipment, television cameras, motion picture projection equipment, and transmitters.

A few young people enter broadcasting with temporary jobs in the summer to replace regular workers on vacation. And others enter the various jobs in the industry without specialized training and later work their way up to positions of responsibility.

And while it is possible to receive training for broadcasting from radio institutes, a liberal arts education with broad knowledge and interest in many fields will give you the best preparation. . . .

Photo/
Urbana student Missionary Convention at the University of Illinois

Those interested in the engineering aspect of broadcasting need to earn a First Class Operator's License from the Federal Communications Commission. Applicants for a license must pass written examinations covering the construction and operation of transmission and receiving equipment, characteristics of electromagnetic waves, and federal government and international regulations and practices covering broadcasting. Information and study guides are available from the Federal Communications Commission, Washington, D.C. 20036.

Says Dr. Eugene R. Bertermann, past president of the National Religious Broadcasters, "We firmly believe that the Lord of the Church has given radio and television broadcasting as twentieth century miracles for the proclamation of His gospel in all the world." Is this where God wants you to serve Him?

[Technicians are needed in many areas of the Christian communications field, and also in nonmedia areas, such as buildings and grounds.]

EDUCATION

"Teachers for the primary and secondary levels are needed in Venezuela" (mission children's school), reads an ad in a missionary magazine. This is a typical call for Christian teachers urgently needed at home and abroad. The rapid growth of the Christian schools movement in the past ten years, with little let-up in sight, gives further impetus to this job market, if the pay scale is not your greatest concern.

No other profession offers so many employment opportunities for women. Women far outnumber men in kindergarten and elementary schools. They hold almost half of the teaching positions in secondary schools and about one-fourth of college and university professorships.

Your possible interest in teaching is directly related to your own school experience of the past ten to twelve years. The more you like school, the more you may find yourself being drawn by the Lord into the teaching profession.

For elementary school teaching, love for and understanding of children is a must. And you'd better be long on patience and self-discipline. The same applies to work with adolescents on the secondary school level. If you teach in a college, you'll focus more on subject matter than on students.

The requirements for teaching at a Christian school on any level are the same for those teaching on secular campuses. For grade school or high school, you'll need at least a bachelor's degree. For work at a Christian college or Bible institute you'll need an M.A. And it would be even better if you went on to earn your Ph.D. degree.

If you have a strong interest in language, social science or history, you'll likely want to teach in one of those areas. But have you considered teaching the Bible or some related subject?

Can you think of greater satisfaction than that which would come to you as a teacher of God's Word?

"There are many ways of doing His work, but it is the same God who does the work in and through all of us who are His," wrote Paul (I Cor. 12:5, *Living Bible*). Perhaps God has a place for you in a Christian organization or will assign you to a church-related vocation.

Excerpted from "The New World of Christian Careers," *Moody Monthly*, June 1972. Used by permission of author.

FREEDOMS

The feel of freedom can leave you buoyant. Some find it in hang gliding. Climbing mountains. Sailing. They absorb it in the air, on land, and at sea.

Right now you may have something of that same feeling. High school is over. The summer lies ahead. In the fall you may take off for some distant campus. Or in the weeks ahead you'll hit the road, or move out of your home into your own apartment.

Such freedoms, like hang gliding, can give you a lift or let you down. You'll have to watch that the wrong currents don't shove you around.

Somehow our most cherished freedoms can dissipate when their spiritual dimensions are ignored. It is true even in the political realm. When Communism substitutes the Almighty State for an Almighty God, freedoms seem to vanish.

The next section not only looks at personal freedom, but also does a little bit of flag-waving, without apology.

You'll read about a man who walked across America, and one who ran across. They both finished their grueling treks convinced that the problems of the human soul, and the problems of the nation's soul, demand spiritual answers.

For that's where the root of all freedoms really lie.

CHAPTER 11

Frauds and Counterfeits

In 1912 near the English hamlet of Piltdown, the discovery of a curious fossil with humanlike cranium and apelike jaw convinced many anthropologists that they had found the long-sought "missing link" between man and ape.

Then in 1953, after more than forty years, new analytic techniques revealed the skull to be a fraud. It had been artificially aged by potassium biochromate.

Further expose of this hoax surfaced only in 1979—with evidence that it had been staged by a leading British scientist of the early 1900s—William Johnson Sollas. It seems he wanted to destroy the reputation of a hated rival scientist, Smith Woodward, by tricking him into publicly accepting as authentic what would later be unmasked as an elaborate joke.

Sollas pulled off the hoax beautifully, but it eventually backfired on him. "The Piltdown man," says *Time* magazine (13 November, 1978), "was accepted not only by Woodward, but by almost the entire scientific establishment." With such eminent names "authenticating" the find, discretion required Sollas to remain mum, for it would have

been "unseemly for a man in his position to admit such a trick."

Because of this professor's prank and the gullibility of scientists determined to prove evolution, millions of schoolchildren for almost a half century were taught that the Piltdown Man was scientific fact. It was quickly pulled from textbooks after the embarrassing discovery in 1953.

The world is full of frauds.

Each year the US government arrests scores of persons who try their hand at making phony money in a basement or a back room. Alert store clerks in time often detect the bogus product, and the manufacturer—if the police can find him—goes off to prison.

The world is full of counterfeits.

Consider two major areas today where many young people, and some older ones too, are falling for the bogus product.

One is in the area of the cults.

Pollster George Gallup, Jr. first gives us the good news.

From his surveys he is persuaded that the evangelical movement today is providing a "powerful thrust" in what may be the "early stage of a profound religious revival"

The world is full of nicely-packaged fake merchanise passed off to you as authentic

throughout the United States.

And on top of that, Harvard sociologist Daniel Bell has predicted that widespread revival of religion throughout all social classes is on its way. Bell links birth pangs of revival to rapid growth of the evangelical, fundamentalist churches.

But wherever the authentic prospers, watch out also for the counterfeit:

Hare Krishna and all the many other forms of Eastern mysticism.

The Jim Joneses.

The "Moonies," and a catalog of other cults.

Those that seem the most flakey or far out may easily turn you off. But some of the other counterfeits may not be so easy to detect.

Some phony paper bills are so unreal that they shout that they're fakes. Others appear so close to the real thing that you're reluctant to admit that the money may be bad.

So it is with the cults.

The more apparent "truth" you find, mixed with the mistakes and error, the more you may want to insist that "they're really OK."

The theology of Sun Myung Moon, for example, mixes conventional Christian concepts, Oriental thought, political ideology, and what "Moonies" believe is "new revelation."

Many of the cults, and even world religions like Islam, borrow certain elements from Christianity. And some of the cults insist they are thoroughly Christian.

But that may be the trap. They'll wave the conventional in their display windows as come-on, and soft-pedal the erroneous elements. Until you join. Then too late you may realize how counterfeit the cult really is.

Many of the cults claim to teach the Bible. If you don't have a firm grip on basic Christian doctrines, they can impress you, perhaps even overwhelm you, with their "knowledge" of the Bible.

But cultists can easily twist the Bible or filter it through their own interpretive writings or the teaching of their own "gurus."

Some cults seem to ooze love, but that too can turn out to be counterfeit. In their group, or "family," they can make you "feel good," especially if your own home life or your relationship with your parents has not been all it should be.

71

Beware of any group that tries to set you against your parents or isolate you from them.

Be cautious about:

Groups that strongly criticize institutional churches or all others but themselves.

Communal living situations (though legitimate Christian communal groups that are above moral and theological reproach do exist).

Strangers who invite you to retreats, free dinners, lectures, even Bible studies, but are evasive about who sponsors them.

Religious leaders who try to exercise tight control over your life, or demand absolute authority over you. Watch out for those who appear preoccupied with power.

The gospel sets you free. Cults enslave. The two are as different as night and day. But you'll have to discern the difference and learn to distinguish the real from the counterfeit (see page 120 for further helps).

The bogus product abounds today in another arena—that of sex.

Counterfeits are all around you.

In his counsel to young evangelicals published in the *Other Side* magazine, Harold Lindsell, editor emeritus of *Christianity Today* magazine, called for "the kind of character that holds nations together."

He sees today, in some circles, "a softness and permissiveness that tolerates almost anything and tends to regard as normative that which Scripture judges abnormal," including premarital sex, homosexuality, and pornography.

History tells us that such sins eventually destroy not only individuals, but even great nations and civilizations.

Despite today's so-called "sexual revolution," many young people, according to figures in a recent Gallup survey, still know in their hearts what is right and what is wrong.

More than four out of every ten outright rejected the idea of sexual freedom. Another 8 percent were not sure. For many others, however, sexual freedom seems very attractive.

But even the term itself is misleading.

There are a growing number of authorities on today's scene, including those who may

have once championed the cause of free sex, who now are telling us that the sexual freedom fling has turned sour, that it not only destroys character, but true love and romance.

And there are also those strong Christian voices, of course, who agree.

Rusty and Linda Wright, a bright young Christian couple who lecture on this controversial subject at universities across the country (she also writes for *Ladies Home Companion*), are reminding their campus audiences that sexual freedom is not all it pretends to be.

Some of those who have tried it now admit they became slaves to their own selfish life-styles.

"On the other hand," say Rusty and Linda in their book *Dynamic Sex* (Here's Life, 1979), "these are some of the tremendous freedoms Jesus Christ offers to those who would follow Him:

"Freedom from anxiety, fear, and guilt about sex. Freedom from slavery to it. Freedom from feeling the need to exploit sex in a relationship. Freedom from pressure to conform to wrong sexual attitudes, values and actions.

"Freedom to relax in the presence of members of the opposite sex. Freedom to accept yourself; to have a positive self-image based on God's love and acceptance rather than on others' evaluations of your worth or sexuality.

"Freedom to trust God to lead you to your life's partner. Freedom to enjoy sex to the utmost, in its proper context (marriage)."

"If therefore the Son shall make you free, you shall be free indeed" (John 8:36).

Even in such a delicate area as sex.

But in today's society, great pressures can force themselves on you. What can you do?

It may be stating the obvious, but a person's conduct and actions, good or bad, always start first in the mind. "As a man thinketh . . . so is he."

The Bible contrasts the carnal-minded and the spiritual-minded, the double-minded and the single-minded, those who habitually think evil and those who think good.

Now to be honest, what kind of signals heavily condition what you think?

What you read.

What you see.

What you hear.

In today's computer language, it's put this way: "Garbage in, garbage out."

That gets to the heart of the matter. Are you in control of the input that is shaping your thoughts, your character, your life?

Or is that input in control of you?

If the latter, that's not freedom. It's counterfeit.

And what spiritual input, if any, are you letting through to counteract the other pressures?

When you get right down to it, you have to do some pretty heavy wrestling with today's media barrage: the books and magazines you read, the TV or theater shows, the radio.

And here's where even our long cherished "freedom of the press," which has been so abused in recent years, can throw you a curve.

The subtle rationale lurking under the surface goes something like this:

If it's on the newsstand, or on the air, or on the TV screen, it's legal. Otherwise the post office, or the FCC, or the network, would have canned it.

If it's legal, it can't be too bad.

Don't fight it (no one likes book burners or censors).

But that line of thinking misses the point.

The world out there is full of both good and evil. You know it, and I know it.

Moreover, the concepts and precepts of law in earlier years were rooted firmly in Judeo-Christian ethics and values. Today much law no longer anchors to any moral law or absolutes.

That's how the Supreme Court was able to permit wholesale abortion (murder before birth). If enough people demand it, they'll probably get it, whether or not it is morally right.

Today a minority of evildoers out to make heavy bucks (the pornographers of all shades, for example) can find all kinds of ways to flout the spirit of the law, but more or less hold to the letter of the law—especially if they print on slick quality paper; use

professional photography; and weave in some legitimate, even sophisticated, quality articles or interviews with respected personalities from the President on down.

Who are they kidding?

The point is, you and I live in a world in which evil can be disguised as legitimate enterprise, and where the media can manipulate the morals of an entire nation, even offend the conscience of the majority, and get away with it.

Moral conditions today might sometimes discourage you, but remember, they were also mighty bad when Paul took on cities like Corinth and even Rome.

So what was his posture and counsel?

He told Christians to let their minds and hearts dwell on that which was good and pure—that is, "Dwell on the fine, good things in others. Think about all you can praise God for and be glad about" (see Philippians 4:8).

But recognize also that sin is very real. Don't ignore it, or excuse it, especially in your own life.

Live "blameless and innocent, children of God above reproach in the midst of a crooked and perverse generation, among whom you appear as lights in the world" (Philippians 2:15).

"Do not be overcome by evil, but overcome evil with good" (Romans 12:21).

Let the Word of God continually cleanse your life, and let the blood of Jesus Christ remove all guilt.

Finally, recognize the ultimate origin of all counterfeits.

Satan is the great cosmic master of deceit, whether it be in the arena of the cults, or sex, or a thousand other areas. His packages often come with attractive wrappings.

Ronald Enroth, author of *Lure of the Cults,* says it well in *Christian Herald* magazine ("Any Preventive for the Cults?" March 1979): "The devil always hides behind a mask; he never carries an ID card."

Don't choose the counterfeits and deprive yourself of all the really good things in life.

by Bill Glass

CHAPTER 12

Thank You, God, for American Youth

Thank you, God, for the young generation and their great preoccupation with freedom; Help them to see that free love is neither free nor love, that freedom of speech is not freedom to prostitute words.

Thanks for their great disillusionment with materialism, but help them to see that America with all her faults has the capability to feed a half-starved world.

Compel them not to risk the American empire with its fantastic potential for good for an opium pipe dream.

Thanks for their zest for pleasure, but may their glands not dominate their brains—to the degree that they would substitute their morality for yours.

And, O God, may this young generation take their mothers and fathers, their brothers and sisters by the hand and lead them to the feet of Jesus where they will discover what peace and freedom really are.

Evangelist Bill Glass was for many years an outstanding pro-football player with the Cleveland Browns. Article used by permission of *The United Brethren* magazine.

CHAPTER 13

In Search of the Real America

On one of North Carolina's Appalachian mountainsides, red-haired Peter Gorton Jenkins, weary from a heavy backpack and a forty-mile hike, eased himself down next to the trunk of a tree. His 100-pound Alaskan malamute, Cooper, stretched out alongside.

Jenkins had set out on foot from his home in south central New York state to discover "the real America." That was shortly after his graduation from college. In his campus years the nation seemed to be falling apart: racial violence, political scandal, student protest. America—should he love it or leave it?

Jenkins decided he would walk from coast to coast, mingle and live among the people, and give America one last chance.

After several months on the trail, Jenkins saw hope. In his story for *National Geographic*, later packaged into a best-selling book *(A Walk Across America)*, he tells the operator of a little country store, "I've come to realize what a bad press America's been giving itself. There's a lot of good in it that also needs telling. The land, the geography—they're unbelievable. And the people! I haven't gone a day that someone I met

hasn't been kind, or thoughtful, or helpful. Plain, simple ordinary folks they may be, but they're heroes to me."

No, America is not perfect. She still has inflation, unemployment, her occasional scandals, fuel shortages, and pockets of poverty.

There is even a crack in her liberty bell.

But half the world goes to bed hungry, and half the world lies behind iron and bamboo curtains where freedom, as Americans know it, just does not exist.

Homemakers in more needy parts of the world might never see in a lifetime the quantity of food from which the American housewife can choose while shopping at a supermarket.

So far America has escaped the specter of wide scale hunger at home, and she has been able to feed, at times, at least some of the hungry abroad.

In spite of her social ills, the US has passed more social legislation and enacted more laws providing individual liberty than any other nation in world history.

And because of her belief in freedom of the press, she has not hidden her scars—they

One of them walked across the land; another ran. They both concluded that the problems of our nation, at their deepest levels, demand spiritual answers

are out in the open for the world to see—while those totalitarian regimes that run a controlled press look on amazed at her candor.

Like no other nation America still serves as a "melting pot" for peoples of the world, and the extent to which hundreds of thousands even today, from Cuba to Laos, seek freedom within her shores, speaks loudly against her critics.

But the great privileges we enjoy should make us stop to think. Do we really understand the roots of these freedoms? And are we in danger of losing the freedoms we enjoy by softness, ignorance, or default?

A nation that enjoys prosperity must face the dangers of it. Serious questions arise:

Does material abundance of itself produce the kind of national character that counts most?

How will the have-not nations react in the immediate years ahead?

Should affluent Americans feel guilty over this disparity?

To this last question some say yes, and point to the many Scriptures that clearly reveal an obligation to the poor.

Others say no. It is impossible, they insist, for America to feed the whole world. The crisis can never be resolved, they say, until those nations put free enterprise into action and remove some of the faulty foundations, both economic and religious, that have helped to create their own catastrophes.

Both sides make a point, and the real answer probably lies somewhere in between.

In concern for economic justice, some at this point entertain a faulty and dangerous option.

They decide to blend in a little Marxism.

Harold Lindsell of *Christianity Today* magazine warns flatly, "One cannot extract aspects of Marxist thought from its total setting without doing violence to the distinctive Christian world and life view" (Harold Lindsell, "Think on These Things—Advice to Young Evangelicals," *The Other Side,* March-April 1975).

Sooner or later the state replaces God, and freedom vanishes.

If you begin to feel hostile to capitalism, he says, look not at the system itself, but at the people who use or abuse it. The root problem is sin, not the system.

Photo/ Perter Gorton Jenkins and dog Cooper in walk across America

Nor is state socialism the answer.

Charles Colson, author of *Born Again*, and a man who once knew firsthand the extent of government power, now warns that if we docilely accept the propaganda that government can solve all of our problems, we are part and parcel of a "political illusion."

"We must attack modern man's presuppositions," he says in a *National Courier* interview (19 August, 1977), "and expose his myths and illusions for what they are: bankrupt humanist answers to man's dilemmas. We must recognize that we are in spiritual combat; rather than waiting like mindless robots to be programmed by some all knowing, infallible computer called government.

"We as followers of Christ should equip ourselves with the full power of the gospel, assault sin and injustice, compassionately respond to human need and strive to be the salt."

Charles Colson has put his own words into action as a man leading the way in prison reform. There are things about "the system," he believes, that do need to be corrected. But at the core of his program is winning prisoners to Jesus Christ and then helping them to grow.

He already has had enough success that now even some federal prison officials admit that they've seen the gospel accomplish things that all the monies in the federal budget could not have achieved.

Let's look at another example, the story of Tony Ahlstrom.

Tony did not walk across America. He ran.

While a student at an evangelical school in Illinois, Tony was among those concerned about the pollution of our environment.

So in 1970 Tony and his brother, Joel, ran from Chicago to Detroit, carrying a letter from Chicago Mayor Richard Daley to the mayor of Detroit. The result was the passage of a major piece of antipollution legislation in that automotive capital.

It put Tony in touch with Chicago's top city officals, including Mayor Daley and the man who would succeed him.

In 1971 Tony and Joel ran again, this time from Los Angeles to New York, again carrying ecology legislation. The media gave them wide coverage, and they saw legislation passed in cities across the country.

On a third run in 1976, they ran from the Golden Gate Bridge to the White House, fifty-two miles a day, carrying a Bible for then President Gerald Ford and copies of the Declaration of Independence, with thousands of signatures of Americans they met along the way.

But as Tony Ahlstrom saw it, legislation alone was not enough. Our nation's leaders needed the gospel.

So he spent a year in Washington, D.C., making appointments with congressmen (more than one hundred of them). He took each of them a Bible personalized with the congressman's name on the front, looked him in the eye, and clearly and compassionately shared the gospel.

Tony has returned to Chicago, but his energies today still focus on top leaders, as he works particularly with a core of committed Christians on the Chicago city council.

Tony's vision, according to an article in *Moody Monthly* (February 1980) by former NBC newswriter Jan Long Harris, is to see "a group of American leaders meet together after the model of a group in England following John Wesley's revival. Half a dozen members of Parliament would ride out to a country house to discuss and pray about the problems of their day.

"Out of that group came the abolition of child labor, the cleaning up of the gin traffic, and a return to morality in the behavior of the upper classes of society."

Most problems in America, and in the hearts of her citizens, at their deepest levels demand spiritual answers.

Enter again the cross-country nomad, Peter Gorton Jenkins.

Unlike many college graduates, Jenkins had known what "the top" was like.

"I knew powerful corporate executives," he says, "with six-figure incomes who came home at night to drink themselves to sleep. I saw their pampered children applying

Photo/ Tony Ahlstrom

themselves more to drugs than studies while attending elite prep schools.

"I had received graduate scholarship offers plus job offers for fast advancement, but deep down inside I sensed and saw that the answer was not in power, education, money or prestige."

Peter Jenkins began to realize that his trek was a quest not only to find the real America, but to find the very meaning of his existence.

One night in Mobile, Alabama, while on his way to what a friend had said would be a "real wild party," Jenkins saw a sign for a Christian evangelistic crusade. He decided to go.

"Ten thousand people packed the auditorium," describes Jenkins in *National Geographic*. "I sat down front so I could take some pictures, feeling just a bit silly at being there.

"Then up to the podium strode the evangelist, a tall, tough Texan who looked more like a linebacker for the Dallas Cowboys than a preacher. But a preacher he was."

At the close of the meeting, Jenkins and some three hundred others walked to the podium at the evangelist's invitation.

" 'Do you accept Jesus as your personal saviour?' he asked us.

"My lips opened. I said I did. I meant it.

"Again he asked, again each of us replied, affirming our acceptance.

"Later, relaxed and clear-eyed and more inwardly at peace than I had ever been, I floated out of there and back into the street.

"I never did get to that real wild party."

Quotations by Peter Gorton Jenkins, "Walk Across America," *National Geographic Magazine*, April 1977, are reprinted by permission of the author.

CHAPTER 14

In Search of Our "Roots"

The famous pony express of yesteryear whisked the mail across the western wilderness from St. Louis to Sacramento in just ten days.

But it took an elaborate relay system to make it work, complete with four hundred horses, some eighty young riders, plus station keepers, stock tenders, route superintendents, and shuttling supply wagons.

Over that historic rugged trail of 1,840 miles, the mail changed hands no less than 157 times.

Yet it inevitably made it through.

It could never have happened had there not always been a rider at the next station, ready to grab the mail sack, thunder the next five to twenty miles, and in turn pass it on.

When the apostle Paul answered the Macedonian call (Acts 16:10), he planted the gospel in Europe and started a "gospel relay express," so to speak, that has lived on down through the centuries.

That's the way it is with the gospel. It always takes someone to pass it on.

Historical evidence suggests that the gospel may have advanced as far north as Scotland even as early as the first century.

And the man who evangelized what is now Ireland, they say, was none other than "St. Patrick" himself.

In reality, he was a first-century fundamentalist, on fire for the Lord, who passed on the true faith centuries before churches in other parts of the world sent missionaries to Europe.

From that toehold, church historians now tell us, evangelicalism took root in Europe. Not to be snuffed out, it lived on through the centuries, though in low profile at times, and ultimately provided the fuel for the Reformation.

The very same evangelicalism set the stage for the early settling of America.

Strange, isn't it, how history works?
Or God?

There were always those on hand at the strategic moment, it would seem, who understood the gospel in its purity and were ready to pass it on.

Take the Pilgrims, for example.

They left Europe to get out from under its stifling religious and political atmosphere. In the New World they could worship the Lord

The famous pony express relayed the mail across 1,840 miles. Christians have relayed their message across twenty centuries

and obey the Scriptures as they saw them, without interference or compromise.

Enough of the king and the king's church, they said.

It so happens they took aboard a contingent of nonbelievers, or "strangers," who did not share their strong religious conviction.

But the party that landed at Plymouth Rock that bleak November day in 1620 was thoroughly in the hands of evangelicals.

The famed Mayflower Compact, which they all signed aboard ship just before landing, to keep peace and order once on shore, contributed significantly to the political foundations of our republic.

The diary of the Pilgrims, kept by William Bradford, is saturated with the spiritual insight, faith, love, and prayers of that bold Christian group.

God had preserved for them an almost untouched continent, where they could make a new start, exercise their faith freely, and immediately begin to pass it on.

Enter next the Puritans, who established their colony on Massachusetts Bay. Like our other forefathers, they were not perfect, but in general historians have done them injustice. They were in many ways the progressives of their day.

From the outset the Puritans stressed education. Only five years after they established the Massachusetts Bay Colony, the Puritans launched in Boston the first elementary school supported directly by public taxes.

They also planted grammar schools in every town of more than one hundred families. And they put the Bible in the center of the curriculum.

Of some twenty thousand colonists who made their way across the Atlantic to this New England colony, perhaps less than one-fifth even professed to be Christians.

But it was the Puritans who immediately took charge and established the government, built the schools, administered the churches, and set the colony's moral tone.

The Puritans saw themselves essentially as "a people of Israel in the American wilderness," and so they set out to model their Massachusetts colony along biblical lines.

Puritan New England strongly helped shape the foundations of the nation to come. Men like John Cotton, Increase Mather, and scores of others preached forcefully from her pulpits.

Those were people who knew how to pass it on.

But the influx of new settlers each year, along with other pressures, gradually eroded the foundations of this Bible commonwealth. And there arose voices—even voices of dedicated Christians—who thought that such a commonwealth ought not to be imposed on the entire populace.

In fact, they saw it as a threat both to good government and to good Christianity.

Let there be, they said, a separation of church and state.

Next came a new breed of Christian, epitomized by the outspoken Roger Williams of Rhode Island, who founded the first Baptist church in America.

Williams challenged the basis of the Massachusetts Bay government. He argued for a compact theory of government that rested entirely on "the consent of the governed."

He contended that good civil government and also a vigorous Christian faith could indeed flourish in a land that allowed religious liberty for all.

Williams and those likeminded were not trying to free themselves or the people from a fervent Christian faith. In fact, they saw personal evangelism as a matter of first priority.

But they were also intelligent enough to see that another church-state system could be a noose around everyone's neck.

In fact, was that not the very thing many of the first settlers had sought to escape by fleeing Europe?

Soon another great drama began: The evangelical movement of precolonial years paved the way for the American Revolution itself.

The role played by evangelicals in preparing the country for independence is "one of the best kept secrets in American history," according to author Sherwood Wirt ("From Revival to Revolution," *Christian Herald*, July-August 1977).

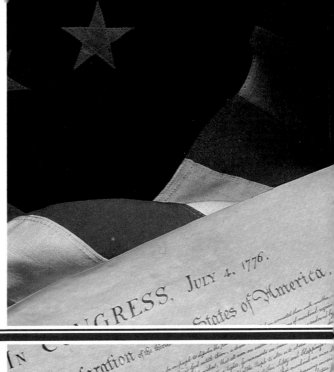

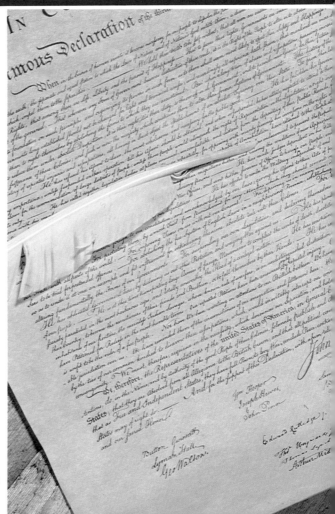

Much of the impetus for freedom had its roots in a remarkable movement of God called the "Great Awakening," which took hold under the preaching of a former Yale graduate and later Princeton president, Jonathan Edwards.

Most historians agree that Jonathan Edwards stands with Benjamin Franklin as one of the two outstanding minds in eighteenth century America.

The great New England revival began in 1734, while Jonathan Edwards was preaching a series of sermons on justification by faith alone. Conversions began, first with the young, then among older ones. A notorious young woman was saved. It was like a "flash of lightening" to the young people.

By 1736 Edward's church in Northampton had three hundred new converts, and news of the revival had spread throughout New England.

But it took a new surge when George Whitefield arrived from England in 1740 for two years of evangelism in America.

During the years 1740-42, some 25,000 to 50,000 people were added to New England churches, out of a total population at that time of 300,000. God reached out and touched at least one of every six lives in that awakening.

Under the preaching of Gilbert Tennant and others, the revival spread rapidly southward into the Middle Atlantic colonies.

Thousands responded to God, and preachers, along with the masses of ordinary Christians, passed it on.

It was a great spiritual event in the annals of American history.

Eventually it also turned out to leave a strong political impact.

The religious tone of America at that time, some say, was one of the prime causes of the Revolution. When people have religious liberty, they also expect political liberty.

Not all colonial Christians, especially those loyal to the Anglican church, backed the Revolution. Citing passages like Romans 12, they even saw it as contrary to Scripture.

But the voices of freedom overruled. Some have even said that it was evangelicalism that inspired and molded the free institutions of the United States.

And it was the evangelists, says Sherwood Wirt, "who, more than any other people, welded the colonies into a psychological and spiritual unity.

"Whitefield in particular unified the colonists simply by uniting them into Christ wherever he went. He introduced many of the leaders of the different colonies to each other, for he knew them all, having traveled the length of the Atlantic seaboard many times. Thus he helped to create a common American spirit, which became the spirit of '76."

Colonial leaders emerged as the product of evangelical churches. The Bible was read more than any other book. Christians planted new colleges.

But nearly one hundred years after the First Great Awakening in America, God had to step in again.

By now the nation was much larger, both in numbers and territory. Many of the people were pushing westward by wagon across the Appalachians and onto the rugged frontier.

It took all their energies just to hack out their farms in the forests and then survive. For many, religion took a back seat, if it had even gotten aboard the wagon at all.

During that time the "farmer-preacher," usually a Baptist, was introduced.

This individual, ordained or licensed to preach, took up farming right along with the other frontiersmen. He cleared and worked his land like his neighbors, became the shepherd of the little Baptist flock, and conducted the "religious meetin's" on Sundays or as the need arose.

Many of those farmer-preachers, although lacking formal education and salaried positions, were greatly used of God.

They too "passed it on."

Also in that period arose the circuit rider, usually a Methodist.

These hardy men established themselves as front-runners in bringing the gospel to the frontier. They preached a simple message of free grace, won converts by the thousands, and spread revival.

By 1830 there were more than one-half million converts.

One such circuit rider was Francis Asbury.

For nearly forty years he rode the wilderness in nineteen states, over mountains, steep hills, deep rivers, and muddy creeks, telling people of salvation in Jesus Christ.

On occasions too numerous to count, his life hung by a thread, as he fought rain, cold, snow, disease, wild animals, and other perils.

"I consider myself in danger," he once wrote in his diary, "but my God will keep me whilst thousands pray for me."

It is estimated that during his career he covered no less than 250,000 miles. On horseback!

The circuit rider refused to hole up in the safety of a comfortable church, or in a home, at least for very long. He was out there year after year, with Bible and tracts, seeking out back trails and homestead cabins buried in the wilderness.

He went to where the people were. He too knew how to pass it on.

Photo/ Early circuit riders

Many believe the Second Great Awakening helped reverse the nations' spiritual skid and surely saved America from future judgment and calamity.

Where did it start?

Some say among a few families and small churches in the backwoods of North Carolina. When those little congregations moved west into Logan County, Kentucky, they took the small spark of revival with them. And in time it began to spread.

It was then that the historical "camp meeting" emerged.

As word of revival spread, Kentuckians from as far as one hundred miles threaded their way to the meetings. Crowds grew. Soon visitors had to camp out for one, two, or three nights.

Men chopped down more trees to accommodate the crowds and arranged split-long benches into a veritable church-in-the-wilderness.

The Cane Ridge meeting extended over several days in August 1801 and drew crowds estimated as high as 25,000.

Despite emotional excesses, and the criticism that ensued, the revival movement continued to spread and ultimately made a profound impact on the lives and morals of western society at that time.

In later years the camp meeting took on much more orderly form. It continued to be a means of proclaiming the gospel and passing it on.

The camp meeting, in fact, laid the foundations of mass evangelism, which later took on a much more sophisticated tone.

Again, in the decades after the Second Great Awakening, God used evangelists like Dwight L. Moody, Charles Finney, and Billy Sunday to reach literally millions of people with the gospel of Jesus Christ.

D.L. Moody preached to millions not only in the US, but also in Great Britain.

It is estimated that the preaching of Finney influenced change in one-half million lives. At Rochester, New York, alone, during 1830, one hundred thousand made profession of faith in Jesus Christ.

In 1917 Billy Sunday, Chicago pro-baseball-player turned evangelist, preached to a million and a half in New York during a ten-week campaign.

They were merely the catalysts God used to stir hundreds of thousands of others also to go out and make Jesus Christ known. Another generation rose up to pass it on.

Behind history, it seems, is a coherent plan after all and a stream of events that begin to make sense when you back off far enough and take a wide view.

And if you are a Christian, you can be especially grateful for the long line of witnesses who relayed the message.

But what of today?

Your generation and mine are still passing on the gospel—by television, satellite, radio, and all the traditional ways that have worked for centuries.

It happens every day—on the campus, in church, at home, or on the job.

"One generation shall praise thy works to another" (Psalm 145:4).

Ordinarily, that means you are expected to pass the torch to the generation to follow you. That will eventually include your own children.

But history reveals that revival, even among the populace as a whole, often starts with young people.

Regardless of age, the gospel can move both ways.

So did that mail once carried by the pony express.

The relay is not yet over.

Be sure you pass it on.

How Evangelicals Launched the Ivy League

Only eighteen years after the Pilgrims set foot on Plymouth Rock, the Puritans established Harvard. Its "rules and precepts" adopted in 1646 included the following essentials:

"Every one shall consider the main end of his life and studies to know God and Jesus Christ which is eternal life.

"Seeing the Lord giveth wisdom, every one shall seriously by prayer in secret seek wisdom of him.

"Every one shall so exercise himself in reading the Scriptures twice a day that they be ready to give an account of their proficiency therein, both in theoretical observations of languages and logic, and in practical and spiritual truths."

More than half of the seventeenth-century Harvard graduates became ministers.

In 1701 Yale was launched by Christians as an alternative to Harvard, when the spiritual climate of the latter school began to decline.

1746: Princeton sprang up in part from the impact of the First Great Awakening, or the great New England revival. It retained its evangelical vigor longer than any of the other Ivy League schools.

1754: Dartmouth began as a missionary school designed to evangelize the Indians and also to Christianize English youth.

The first president of New York's Columbia University was an outstanding Christian and former missionary, Dr. Samuel Johnson.

Brown University originated with the Baptist churches scattered along the Atlantic seaboard.

With the exception of Cornell and the University of Pennsylvania, evangelicals started every school in what is today know as "the Ivy League."

Yet even the original building at the University of Pennsylvania was constructed specifically to accommodate the great outdoor preaching of evangelist George Whitefield.

His statue still stands on the campus today.

When the Ivy League schools eventually secularized, and evangelical fervor waned, a new wave of Christian schools emerged from the American soil in the late 1800s to fill the vacuum. Among the earlier ones were Nyack Missionary school in New York state, Wheaton College, and the Moody Bible Institute.

Today the Christian college movement in the US enrolls in the tens of thousands.

If you are a student in one of these evangelical schools, your campus roots, in a very real sense, go back to the early days of the Ivy League.

THE GOD WHO IS THERE

Man probes into space. Through telescopes. Radioastronomy. Space rockets—with their sophisticated photo feedbacks—that streak by Mars and Venus, and speed beyond. So far out there. Yet only the beginning of the universe.

When the Russians first chased into space and back, they reported—almost gleefully—that they had not found God. But when US astronaut James Irwin stood on the moon and looked back at planet Earth, he sensed God's presence in such a profound way that he resolved right there to evangelize once he returned home. He has done just that.

A handful flatly shout there is no God. But the atheists are few. Others say they just don't know, and call themselves agnostics. An overwhelming majority of Americans insist that God does indeed exist. But not all of those, by far, know how to make Him real in their daily lives.

How you view God in your own life may reflect in part how great you realize His universe, and His attributes, to be. But you must also meet Him in the Man, Jesus Christ. The One who once came down to earth, and died, and rose again.

The Man who always was. The Man who will also come back.

Is it time to stretch your mind, open your heart, and discover anew the God who is there?

96

15

Scientists on a Star Trek

During lonely nighttime vigils as a shepherd, David wrote: "The heavens declare the glory of God and the firmament showeth his handiwork" (Psalm 19:1). David's vision was limited to four or five thousand stars. Today's astronomer sees or has evidence of almost numberless galaxies.

What is the evidence for God's existence, glory, and handiwork perceived by present-day observers of the heavens?

Writing in the *New York Times Magazine* [later reprinted in *Readers Digest*], Robert Jastrow,*director of NASA's Goddard Institute for Space Studies and author of *Until the Sun Dies,* asks the exciting question: "Have Astronomers Found God?"

"It should be understood from the start that I am agnostic in religious matters," Dr. Jastrow says. "However, I am fascinated by some strange developments going on in astronomy—partly because of their religious implications and partly because of the peculiar reactions of my colleagues."

What are these "strange developments"? That the universe had, in some sense, a

beginning—that it began at a certain moment in time and under circumstances that seem to make it impossible—not just now, but ever—to find out what force or forces brought the world into being at that moment. Was the creative agent one of the familiar forces of physics, or was it, as the Bible says, "Thine all-powerful hand that creates the world out of formless matter?"

"The general scientific picture that leads to the big-bang theory is well-known. We have been aware for 50 years that we live in an expanding universe, in which all the galaxies around us are moving apart from us and one another at enormous speeds. The universe is blowing up before our eyes, as if we are witnessing the aftermath of a gigantic explosion.

"Now we see how the astronomical evidence leads to a biblical view of the origin of the world (the word the Bible used to describe the universe). The details differ, but the essential elements in the astronomical and biblical accounts of Genesis are the same: the chain of events leading to man

*Robert Jastrow, "Have Astronomers Found God?" *New York Times Magazine*, 25 June 1978. © 1978 by The New York Times Company. Reprinted by permission.

Astronomers who had long explained the universe as a long "process of evolution" now are puzzled by evidence that it may have started instantaneously

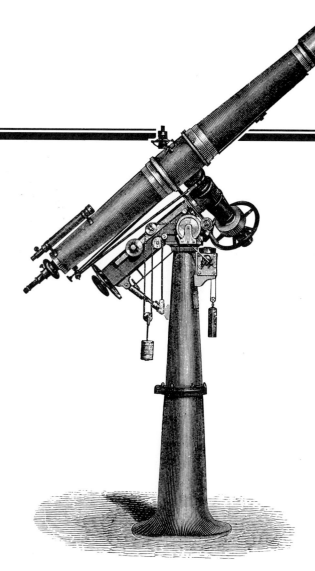

commenced suddenly and sharply at a definite moment in time, in a flash of light and energy."*

Dr. Jastrow says that theologians are "predictably delighted" with the proof (his word) that the universe had a beginning. Astonomers, on the other hand, are "curiously upset." Their reactions provide an interesting demonstration of the response of the scientific mind—supposedly a very objective mind—when evidence uncovered by science itself leads to a conflict with the articles of faith in our profession.

It turns out that the scientist behaves the way the rest of us do when our beliefs are in conflict with the evidence. We become irritated, we pretend the conflict does not exist, or we paper it over with meaningless phrases.

Albert Einstein was one who became "annoyed" at the new development, according to Dr. Jastrow—even though his theory of relativity predicted the basic fact of an exploding universe. The German chemist Hermann Nernst wrote, "To deny the infinite

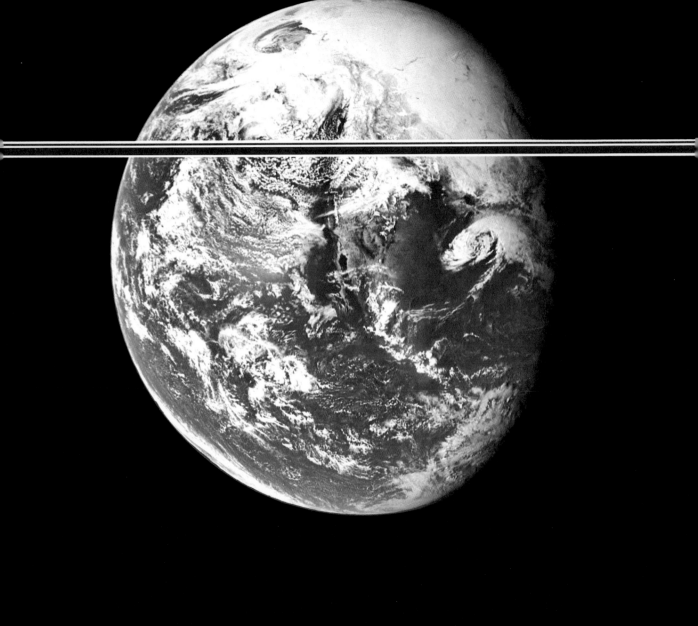

SCIENTIFIC CREATIONISM

duration of time would be to betray the very foundations of science."

More recently, Philip Morrison of M.I.T. said he "would like to reject" the big-bang theory. And Allan Sandage of Palomar Observatory said, "It is such a strange conclusion . . . it cannot really be true."

Why these emotional reactions? Dr. Jastrow gives us his own explanation of the unscientific response. "I think part of the answer is that scientists cannot bear the thought of a natural phenomenon that cannot be explained, even with unlimited time and money. There is a kind of religion in science; it is the religion of a person who believes there is order and harmony in the universe, and every event can be explained in a rational way as the product of some previous event; every effect must have its cause.

"Einstein wrote, 'The scientist is possessed by the sense of universal causation.' This religious faith of the scientist is violated by the discovery that the world had a beginning under conditions in which the known laws of physics are not valid, and as a product of forces or circumstances we cannot discover. When that happens the scientist has lost control. If he really examined the implications, he would be traumatized. As usual when faced with trauma, the mind reacts by ignoring the implications—in science this is known as 'refusing to speculate'—or trivializing the origin of the world by calling it the big-bang, as if the universe were a firecracker."

I find Dr. Jastrow's final conclusion delightful: "At this moment it seems as though science will never be able to raise the curtain on the mystery of Creation. For the scientist who has lived by his faith in the power of reason, the story ends like a bad dream. He has scaled the mountains of ignorance; he is about to conquer the highest peak; as he pulls himself over the final rock, he is greeted by a band of theologians who have been sitting there for centuries."

Reprinted from *Eternity* magazine, December 1978. Used by permission of author.

by Nancy Barcus
with Dick Bohrer

CHAPTER 16

Christians vs. Humanists

When you hear warnings to beware of secular humanism, take note. Secular humanists believe your faith is outdated. They mean to convince you to give it up. This is a new kind of humanism—unlike its gentle predecessor, cultural humanism, which simply urged appreciation for man's achievements. Should you meet up with a secular humanist, think long and hard.

Secular humanists are as organized as the evangelical church, they are funded, and they even have a "Bible," called the Humanist Manifesto.

Humanists have set themselves an impressive task—to dissuade God-believers from their faith because they are convinced "belief in God is the highest form of self-deception."

"Do we need traditional Christianity?" they ask in their magazine, *The Humanist* (March-April 1980, p. 43).

In that article writer Ernest Morgan replies: No.

"Once God was a big, strong man with a beard, generally invisible, who ran the show. He chose as his people—if we are to believe the Bible—a warlike Bedouin tribe that energetically raveged its neighbors under his instructions.

"As human knowledge increased, such a God became less and less credible, and God gradually became a symbol" (p. 156).

They believe that man is alone in this universe.

The Humanist Manifesto, first drawn up in 1933 and updated in 1973, declares, "We can discover no divine purpose or providence for the human species. . . . No deity will save us; we must save ourselves. . . . Promises of immortal salvation or fear of eternal damnation are both illusory and harmful."

University of Buffalo (NY) Professor Paul Kurtz, editor of *The Humanist,* says in that magazine's November-December 1978 issue: "Humanism cannot, in any fair sense of the word, apply to one who still believes in God as the source and creator of the universe. . . ."

Christian students must prepare themselves to face such challenges. They must know the difference between the "humanism" that

Behind evolution, the "sex revolution," and much of secular education lies humanism, which would remove God and put man at the center of all

covers anything from appreciation for the arts to concern for their fellow man (which is legitimate) and this special category called "secular humanism" (which entirely leaves God out).

Secular humanist dogma reflects the mind-set of unsaved man. Christians would all do well to master the following arguments which refute the cardinal doctrines of secular humanism:

CREATION AND THE UNIVERSE

● Humanists believe the world was formed from chaos and is itself chaos except as man's reason finds ways to organize it. There is no divine purpose or plan.

Christians believe there is an observable order to creation from sub-atomic particles to highest forms, evidencing a responsible Higher Intelligence.

● Humanists believe that if we find any plan or consistency in the universe, it is due to natural processes of evolution that can take many turns since there is no God directing them.

Christians believe consistency throughout the universe is of such a high order that men on earth can compute mathematically the course of a rocket and find the laws of nature in accordance with those formulas. This consistency from sphere to sphere is too broad-based to have emerged from chaos.

GOD

● Humanists insist that since no master-Mind created the universe, there is no personal God who gives meaning to existence.

Christians insist man's yearning for meaning is satisfied only by the companionship of a personal God who *is* life. Psychological breakdown and despair are phenomena of the twentieth century when God disappeared from common thinking.

● Humanists believe that no God oversees or organizes the course of history. Man makes of history what he *sees* fit—without a master plan. He is not responsible to any higher Power or Law. All his plans and programs are designed with the interest of human individuality alone as their goal.

Photo/ Madalyn Murray tears up a Bible during debate

103

Christians believe that from the Book of Genesis to the present, nations that fail to respect God slip into individualistic self-interest, hedonism—that doctrine holding that pleasure or happiness is the sole good in life—and finally into decay.

Interestingly, the highly authoritarian regimes of the Russian and Communist Chinese governments resist the sin of hedonism by imposing cruel restraints on the operation of human nature. The bankruptcy of the human personality without God is still the result.

MAN

● Humanism holds that man is an "accident of chemistry."

Christianity holds that man is too well organized as a biological and intellectual masterpiece to be an accident. The statistical probability against his accidental occurring evidences divine engineering.

● Humanists believe the mind of man is the key to a better world. "Reason and intelligence are the most effective instruments

that mankind possesses" (Humanist Manifesto II).

Christians believe faith in reason and in the scientific method alone is naive. The mind calculates imperfectly, supplanting theory with theory, for each man is imprisoned in his own subjective "pair of glasses." Reason and intelligence are useful, but not entirely trustworthy.

● Humanists believe compassion and our working together for a humane world will bring progress.

Christians believe selfishness affects our ability to act consistently, even though we wish to. We stumble over our own inner motives and over the law of sin outlined in Romans 7. Our efforts to save the world are continuously confounded by the selfish counterplays of human nature.

We need a Savior and the Holy Spirit to make us compassionate and effective.

● Humanists believe man will be happy when he achieves economic well-being in a world of "shared human values."

Christians believe economic well-being does not make men nicer or good—as

American affluence will attest. "Shared human values" cannot be defined except as "the good of the greatest number." But what is good? Without God, no definite answer is available; only vague phrases appear in humanist documents.

● Humanists believe happiness on this earth is all men can hope for.

Christians believe hope of eternal life provides higher incentives and vision for human action of earth. "Now we see through a glass darkly; but then face to face" (1 Cor. 13:12).

MORALITY

● Humanism holds that there is no absolute good or evil.

But Christians can insist from Scripture that real good and real evil have been clearly understood by even the most primitive cultures (Rom. 1:18-20).

● Humanists believe all acts are morally neutral, except for their influence on others for good or ill.

Christians believe acts are *not* morally neutral. The Ten Commandments in the Old Testament and Christ's higher laws in the New supply absolutes of truth we understand every time we break them. The consequences are shattered lives.

● Humanists believe man can create a standard of right and wrong as he goes along, changing the rules whenever necessary to get rid of "old fashioned ideas" like sexual continence. Toleration is a virtue.

Christians believe that old-fashioned ideas like sexual morality work better than the new ideas. Physical sex symbolizes the highest human relationship—marriage and trust between man and woman. The "new freedom" has debased this view of sex and has substituted hedonism as the norm.

Toleration is a virtue only if balanced with discernment of the consequences of one's ideas and of the accountability of the individual to God.

● Humanism promises a world where "peace, prosperity, freedom, and happiness are widely shared." But it does not provide any method or tool except trust in man to achieve this end. It says, "Humans are responsible for what we are or will be" (Humanist Manifesto II).

Christianity offers "peace, prosperity, freedom, and happiness" in Christ. It provides answers to "Who am I?" and "How can I be better?": Be redeemed by faith in the substitutionary death of Christ (Rom. 5:6-8; Titus 3:5-7; 1 Cor. 5:17; Gal. 6:14-15).

Christianity answers the rationalist's question, "How can a good God make such a cruel world?" with the answer of human freedom and the fall of man—a carefully thought-out position from Scripture. Rationalism simply ignores the question and then blames the Christian for not easily answering it.

Christianity, unlike rationalism, takes into account the human personality with its deep longing for truth, identity, and the explanation of its Source.

Christians believe that acts have consequences, a position more in line with the givens of human experience than the "it doesn't matter what I do, if it makes everybody happy" attitude. Broken and pained individuals world-wide witness to this fact.

Christians look to a Creator-God, a Redeemer-God, a Spirit-filling God to sustain them in this venture of life, now and evermore.

Humanists call this "folly."

And sadly reveal their own.

CHAPTER 17

by Bill Bright

The Greatness of God

Would you like to live a joyful, abundant and fruitful life—every day filled with adventure? You can.

You start by getting to know God—who he is and what he is like—because your concept of God influences every area of your life: it determines how you relate to yourself, other people, and every circumstance you encounter.

Do you feel shy, unworthy? A right view of God will change your attitude toward yourself.

Do you hold grudges and resent other people? Recognizing God's love and forgiveness toward you will cause you to love and forgive others.

Are you confronted with problems that seem insurmountable? A person with a proper perspective of God's majesty and magnificence can face difficulties with a thankful and trusting spirit.

In his book, *The Knowledge of the Holy,* A. W. Tozer says, "What comes into our minds when we think about God is the most important thing about us. We tend by a secret law of the soul to move toward our mental image of God."

Do you think God is like a divine Santa Claus? A cosmic policeman? A dictator? A big bully?

King David had the right perspective of God. In Psalm 145:1-7 he wrote: "I will praise you, my God and King, and bless your name each day and forever. Great is Jehovah! Greatly praise him! His greatness is beyond discovery! Let each generation tell its children what glorious things he does. I will meditate about your glory, splendor, majesty, and miracles. Your awe-inspiring deeds shall be on every tongue; I will proclaim your greatness. Everyone will tell about how good you are, and sing about your righteousness."

David's God was the infinite God of the universe, mighty in power and worthy of his trust.

I am personally persuaded that if we were to spend more time in the presence of God, worshiping him, praising him, adoring him, reading his Word and talking with him in prayer, our faith and witness would be multiplied many times.

Your problems with people, or with yourself, may stem from your inadequate concept of God

Consider some of the attributes of God—those characteristics that God has disclosed to be true of himself:

God is *eternal*. God has said in his Word, "I am the Alpha and the Omega" (Rev. 1:8)—the beginning and the ending of all things. The psalmist describes God's eternalness this way: "Before the mountains were created, before the earth was formed, you are God without beginning or end" (Ps. 90:2).

We are like people who are watching the parade of history though a keyhole. All we see are people passing by that keyhole, one or two at a time. But God is, for the sake of this illustration, on a mountain and sees the parade begin and end. With him there is no such thing as time.

God is also *omnipresent*. He is not limited in space; he is everywhere. Not only is God *with* us, but he also *indwells* us as believers.

I can catch a plane and fly to far-off countries; but no matter where I go, God is with me. There are times of testing, times of temptation, times of adversity, but God is there. He is there in his love to comfort, he is there in his wisdom to give counsel, he is there in his strength to give support.

Wherever you are or whatever your need, God is there to help you. He is nearer than our hands and feet, closer than our breathing. We can't escape him. God reminds us in Jeremiah 23:23, 24: "Am I God who is only in one place and cannot see what they are doing? Can anyone hide from Me? Am I not everywhere in all of heaven and earth?"

In Psalm 139:6-10 we read: "This is too glorious, too wonderful to believe! I can never be lost to your Spirit! I can never get away from God. If I go up to heaven, you are there; if I go down to the place of the dead, you are there. If I ride the morning winds to the farthest oceans, even there your hand will guide me, your strength will support me."

Another attribute of God is his *omniscience*. He knows everything. David says in Psalm 139:1-4, "O Lord, you have examined my heart and know everything about me. You know when I sit or stand. When far away, you know my every thought. You chart the path ahead of me, and tell me where to stop and rest. Every moment, you know where I am. You know what I am going to say before I even say it."

There is nothing about us that remains unknown to him; every sin, failure, and weakness is seen and yet he still loves us. What a wonderful God we worship!

The last attribute I want to mention is God's *omnipotence*—his power. He spoke and one hundred billion galaxies were flung into space. Jeremiah talks about God's power in chapter 32, verse 17: "O Lord God! You have made the heavens and earth by your great power; nothing is too hard for you!" And this God loved the world so much that he gave his Son to die on the cross for our sins.

There is no situation or problem in your life that is too difficult for God to handle. The God whom we worship is the One in whom resides all authority. In his hand is supreme power. If only we believed that our God is all-powerful, we would walk with shoulders erect and head held high. We would have great faith in a great God.

There are other equally important attributes of God—his love, faithfulness, goodness, justice, righteousness and many others. Study the Word of God for yourself to find out what God is really like, to fall in love with him and worship him more than you have ever done in the past. Study, memorize, and meditate on the Word of God, and you will learn to trust him more. For "faith comes from hearing and hearing by the word of Christ" (Romans 10:17).

I experience great spiritual benefit by thanking and praising God for who he is and what he does—for his love and forgiveness, for his wisdom and power revealed to us through our Lord Jesus Christ.

Often I pray through Psalm 139; 145-150; Ephesians 3:20-21; Colossians 3; John 14:12; 15:1-8 and other portions of Scripture, praising and worshiping the Lord for his attributes.

As you meditate upon the greatness of God and his promises, your soul will be bathed with his beauty and holiness. And your understanding of God's character will be reflected in your attitudes and actions throughout the day. Like the psalmist, you will want to say: "You have let me experience the joys of life and the exquisite pleasures of your own eternal presence" (Ps. 16:11, [LB]).

Reprinted by permission from *Worldwide Challenge*. Copyright © Campus Crusade for Christ, Inc., 1977.

CHAPTER 18

The Man Who Always Was

Two thousand years have passed since Jesus Christ walked on planet Earth. Today supersonic jets scream across the Atlantic in less time than it probably took the wise men to feed and water their camels.

Men have kicked up dust on the same moon that helped illumine the fields as the shepherds watched over their flocks by night.

Unmanned satellites race toward distant planets whose twinkling light faintly penetrated that dark, agonizing night in the Garden of Gethsemane, where the One who sweat great drops of blood moved deliberately toward the cross and changed the course of history.

Why should the Jesus of those days so long ago have any appeal to this modern generation? That's what some of the critics would ask.

Yet the Bible continues to be a best-seller. Churches grow. Young people talk of Jesus in coffee houses, on beaches, on the campus. Bible study groups thrive—in college dormitories, in homes, and on business lunchbreaks. Thousands of Americans, sometimes even those you know, find release from guilt, new meaning to life, perhaps deliverance from drugs. They will never be the same.

But not only in the United States.

Today Christianity is spreading almost like wildfire in some parts of the globe—in Africa, Latin America, and Indonesia. A growing task force continues at the urgent job of translating the Scriptures into new languages and tribal tongues.

It has never been more apparent that Jesus is a Man for all men and all time.

Of course, this is exactly what the Bible foresaw. Millions would follow Him in succeeding centuries. Jesus assured us, "Lo, I am with you always, even unto the end of the age" (Matthew 28:20).

The gospel is for men, everywhere, and throughout all generations!

You may not dispute this, at least in theory. But can you feel it with all your being? Can you see it in the context of your

From the Father above, Jesus came down to planet Earth—a man for all men, all time, all places

life, your friends, your campus, your job, and your ambitions as a graduate?

Pointing others to Jesus is the supreme world cause that holds history together.

For the gospel, you see, cuts across all national boundaries. It also jumps the barriers of age, race, social class, and education. The apostle Paul, a highly educated man, saw himself as "debtor both to the Greeks and to the barbarians; both to the wise and to the unwise" (Romans 1:14). He knew that the gospel was for both the cultured and the un-cultured, the educated and the uneducated.

Jesus Christ is the Man for all men. He leaves no place for tight cliques, snob-bishness, racial prejudice.

Nor does the gospel change with every new political crisis, life-style, or scientific find. No event catches God by surprise.

The Palestine of Jesus' day and our twen-tieth-century scene may seem to be worlds apart. But sin hasn't changed. God hasn't changed. Jesus Christ hasn't changed— neither His judgment nor His love.

David declared that "one generation shall praise thy works to another" (Psalm 145:4). Some in every generation have found that fountain of Life. Your generation must pass it on.

Our Savior never was and never will be confined to time, for He is eternal. Unlike all other religious leaders of world history, He came to earth from outside this planet. He was "with the Father before the world was" (John 17:5). And so will He be forevermore. "I am Alpha and Omega, the beginning and the ending, saith the Lord, who is, and who was, and who is to come, the Almighty" (Revelation 1:8).

In Him lie all the secrets of the universe, the origin of life, the direction of history, the life beyond.

Yes, God loves you. He is there, even when things around you fall apart, or seem chaotic and confused. And He has a plan for your life that He'll reveal to you, step by step, as you seek Him.

by Robert Flood

The Man Who Always Was

In the chaos and confusion
   of a world that wonders why
There is emptiness and loneliness
   and people have to die;
What's our origin, our Future?
Please explain the human race.
Are you out there in the universe,
O God of time and space?

"I am Alpha and Omega,
   the beginning and the ending,"
   saith the Lord, who is, who was,
   and is to come;
"The almighty God who is.
Yes, the Man who always was;
The eternal Jesus Christ who is to come."

There are some who say that
   Jesus lived and died as just a man.
But I know that He existed
   long before the world began;
He has always been alive;
   the Creator is His name
But the world He molded
   didn't recognize Him when He came.

It may seem life has no meaning
   and that history has no goal
But God has a plan for every man
   and still is in control;
And the One who once came down to earth
   and died and rose again
Will come back to reign as King of kings
   and Lord of lords, Amen!

Resources

Guidelist for the Graduate

Here's a select list of goods and services geared especially to the college-bound. Happy hunting!

Agnostics

In contrast to the atheist, who says categorically that there is no God, the agnostic says there may be, but no one can be sure. Read and share with others *The Impossibility of Agnosticism,* by Leith Samuel (Inter-Varsity Press). Booklet reads quickly and is only 35¢.*

America

For fascinating reading on our nation's Christian heritage, read *The Light and the Glory,* by Peter Marshall and David Manuel (Revell). *America: God Shed His Grace on Thee,* by Robert Flood (Moody Press), richly illustrated with graphics, also offers a very readable panorama of evangelicalism in the

US. And for adventure and testimony, join Peter Gorton Jenkins in *A Walk Across America,* a nationwide best-seller now available in paperback (Spire Books).

Athletes

The two major evangelical movements not exclusive within the professional ranks are the Fellowship of Christian Athletes (FCA), 8701 Leeds Road, Kansas City, Missouri 64129; and Athletes in Action (AIA), a division of Campus Crusade for Christ, Arrowhead Springs, San Bernardino, California 92402. Both publish magazines, but the outstanding one is *Athletes in Action* magazine (Here's Life Publishers). It is available only in Christian bookstores or by bulk order. No individual subscriptions.

Bible Atlas

Free, with enrollment in complete Survey of the Scriptures course offered by the Moody Correspondence School, 820 N. LaSalle St., Chicago, Illinois 60610.

---

*Price subject to change.

Bible Memory

Scripture Memory Study Plan, by Bob Seifert (NavPress). Can be used in small-group studies or for individual Scripture study and memorization. Set includes leader's guide, cassette, and workbook, packaged in plastic case. Available at your nearest Christian bookstore, or write NavPress, 3820 N. 30th St./P.O. Box 20, Colorado Springs, Colorado 80901.

Campus Living

HIS Guide to Life on Campus, by Stephen Board. Includes helps on self-identity, spiritual conviction, good study habits, the dating game, and other topics. It's at your Christian bookstore, or write Inter-Varsity Press, Box F, Downers Grove, Illinois 60515.

Campus Movements

The three major interdenominational movements are Campus Crusade for Christ, Inter-Varsity Christian Fellowship, and The Navigators. See profiles on page 31 for further details and their addresses. Why not write each of these organizations for full information, especially if you are headed for a secular university? If possible, let them know the specific campus you will be attending and ask about the ministry there.

Christian Update Forum

At the invitation of Christians on your university campus, and in cooperation with professors, highly qualified Christian educators can be booked to speak in college classrooms and to lecture to the campus at large. In a three-day program, they will bring the Christian view to bear upon a wide span of academic disciplines, such as sociology, psychology, education, physical and natural sciences, anthropology, medical sciences, humanities, history, religion, business, and current issues. Contact Probe Ministries, 12011 Coit Rd., Suite 107, Dallas, Texas 75251.

College Prep

Is there a camp or conference this summer that will give you a Christian orientation to university life, even before you reach the campus? Write the campus movements already mentioned. Or, your home church, along with others, can bring a three-day College Prep seminar (or weekend retreat) right into your own community. Write Probe Ministries, same address as above.

Computer Match

Thousands of openings and opportunities with Christian organizations are waiting for just the right person. To help you match your "profile" (academic, spiritual, job interest, experience) with these positions, write InterCristo, P.O. Box 9323, Seattle, Washington 98109.

Cults

Want help in understanding a particular cult and how to deal with its adherents? In addition to the many good books on the Christian market, you may want to contact The Spiritual Counterfeits Project, P.O. Box 4309, Berkeley, California 94704.

Evolution and Christian answers

The Existence of God and the Creation of the Universe, by William Lane Craig (Here's Life Publishers). *Scientific Creationism,* by Henry M. Morris (Creation-Life Publishers). For information on many other creationist books, and also films, write the Institute for Creation Research (a division of Christian Heritage College), 2716 Madison Ave., San Diego, California 92116.

Films for the Campus

Campus lecturer Josh McDowell has three on the market: *What's Up Josh?*, *The Secret of Loving,* and *More Than a Carpenter.* See your local Christian film rental dealer or write Gospel Films, Inc., Box 455, Muskegon, Michigan 49443. Also, for excellent films on science and faith, ask for a catalog from the Moody Institute of Science, 12000 E. Washington Blvd., Whittier, California 90606.

Magazines

His magazine, published monthly (except summer) by Inter-Varsity. Write *His*, 5206 Main St., Downers Grove, Illinois 60515. *Worldwide Challenge,* published monthly by Campus Crusade for Christ. Christian living, contemporary issues, campus news, Christian work at large, and a regular sports section. Sold in Christian bookstores, or write magazine at Arrowhead Springs, San Bernardino, California 92414.

Missions

Large student missions conference held every two years at the University of Illinois, Urbana. Week-long event between Christmas and New Year's draws capacity registration of around 18,000 from US and abroad. For information on 1981 conference, write Inter-Varsity Missions, 233 Langdon St., Madison, Wisconsin 53703.

Morality

If you, or your friends, are wrestling with issues of the Christian sex ethic for the 1980s, read *Sexual Freedom,* by V. Mary Steward. The author, a young professor of psychology, recounts the sexual revolution that took place in her own life after she became a Christian. Convincing. Inter-Varsity Press booklet. Only 35¢. †

---

†Price subject to change.

Nurses

Nurse's Christian Fellowship (NCF), an affiliate of Inter-Varsity, has chapters on some 160 schools of nursing in the US. Write 233 Langdon St., Madison, Wisconsin 53703. Read also *Spiritual Care: The Nurse's Role* (Inter-Varsity Press).

Quiet Time

NavPress has a little motivational booklet, *Seven Minutes with God,* a devotional diary; and a book, *Appointment with God.* The latter comes with a 30-day workbook. Inter-Varsity Press has a small guidebook, *Quiet Time;* devotions for one year, *This Morning with God;* and a three-year Bible study book, *Search the Scriptures.* Here's Life Publishers has released *Personal Prayer Diary,* assembled by Vonette Bright.

Reason and Faith

Inter-Varsity Press has an impressive line of books and booklets—several hundred. For their latest catalog, address them at Box F, Downers Grove, Illinois 60515. Josh McDowell's *Evidence That Demands a Verdict,* now in paperback, has been a bestseller, and he has written a sequel, *More Evidence That Demands a Verdict.* Also, *Jesus and the Intellectual,* by Bill Bright, is a good, inexpensive little booklet for your intelligent, but perhaps nonbelieving, friends.

Reference Books

Free 16-page catalog of reference books, dictionaries, encyclopedias. Write Reference Book Center, 175 Fifth Ave., New York, New York 10010

Study Bible

Ryrie Study Bible (Moody Press). More than 8,000 helpful footnotes, plus other aids. In King James and New American Standard versions. Available in both cloth and leather (many styles) at your local Christian bookstore.

Credits

Cover Design by Joe Ragont

Cover Photo by H. Armstrong Roberts

The author/compiler expresses special gratitude to Keith Neely, for the graphic design, art and a portion of the photography in GRADUATION—a new start.
—Robert Flood
Olympia Fields, Illinois

Photo Credits

American Motivate, p. 89 right.

Campus Crusade for Christ, pp. 33, 34, 44, 45 left, 52, 64, 65 left, 67.

Decision magazine, p. 45 right.

Flood, David, pp. 51, 61, 87, 90, 7-21, 124.

Flood, Robert, p. 37.

Hartson, Fred, pp. 12, 40, 41, 53, 57, 84, 85, 105.

Harvard University, pp. 31, 39, 95.

Inter-Varsity Christian Fellowship, pp. 4, 7, 32, 33, 43, 62, 63, 65,

McKenzie, F. Joe, p. 88

Moody Monthly, pp. 73, 81, 82, 103.

NASA, pp. 100, 113.

Neely, Keith, pp. 71, 72, 74, 75, 76, 79.

Northwestern University, pp. 27, 28, 36-7, 46-7.

Plymouth Foundation, p. 83.

Sasse, Gene, pp. 13, 15, 23, 35, 56, 58, 59, 77, 104, 107.

Trinity College, Deerfield, p. 66

Wide World Photos, pp. 21-22.

Wheaton College, p. 11.